Wildlife Sound Recording

John B. Fisher
BSc(Eng), MIEE

Foreword by Robert Dougall, MBE

PELHAM BOOKS

To my wife Dora, a fellow enthusiast

First published in Great Britain by PELHAM BOOKS LTD
52 Bedford Square, London WC1B 3EF
1977

ISBN 0 7207 1017 0

Filmset in Great Britain by
Northumberland Press Ltd, Gateshead, Tyne and Wear
and printed by Hollen Street Press Limited,
Slough, Berkshire

Contents

List of Illustrations   6
Foreword   9
Preface   11
Acknowledgements   13

 1 The Lure of Wildlife Sound Recording   15
 2 Identifying Birds from their Sounds *by Alan
    Mitchell*   20
 3 Microphones   39
 4 The Tape Recorder   59
 5 Reflectors   89
 6 Other Field Equipment   104
 7 Field Techniques   111
 8 Stereo Wildlife Sound Recording   126
 9 Some Bird Sounds of Possible Interest *by Alan
    Mitchell*   135
10 Where and When to Record Mammals, Am-
    phibians and Insects   142
11 The Studio   150

Appendices:
 1 Protected Birds   164
 2 Technical Terms   166
    Index   169

List of Illustrations

Photographs

Facing
page

The Sennheiser MKE802 electret gun microphone   32

The author using a Sennheiser gun microphone mounted in its special windshield   32

The Tandberg Series II portable recorder   33

The Nagra ISD portable recorder   33

The Uher CR210 compact cassette recorder   64

The Uher 4200 Report IC reel-to-reel portable recorder   64

Hand holding a reflector; the author demonstrating home-made equipment   65

Using a mono-pod reflector mount   65

The author observing a colony of black-headed gulls on a moorland tarn   96

Bempton Cliffs, Yorkshire – a good area for recording kittiwake, fulmar, guillemot, razorbill, puffin and gannet   96

Leighton Moss, Lancashire – the haunt of bittern, water rail, teal, and many other interesting species   97

Surrey heathland – the habitat of nightingale, night-jar, stonechat, etc 97

The starling – a bird which well repays recording 128

The common toad – its soft call presents a challenge to the recordist 128

The grey squirrel – a suggested subject for study 129

Recording insects with the aid of a sound-proof chamber 129

Line Drawings

page

1 Frequency response curve 43
2 Polar diagram 51
3 Matching microphones to a high input impedance recorder with long microphone leads 57
4 Balanced and unbalanced microphone connections 58
5 Recorder amplifiers 70
6 Graphical illustration of DC bias 75
7 Tape head pre-amplifier equalized to CCIR playback at 190 mm/s. 86
8 Properties of the parabola 90
9 Frequency response of omni-directional microphone in 609 mm (24 in.) diameter reflector of 178 mm (7 in.) focal length 92
10 Frequency response of omni-directional microphone in 457 mm (18 in.) and 304 mm (12 in.) diameter reflectors of 178 mm (7 in.) focal length 93
11 Frequency response of omni-directional microphone in 609 mm (24 in.) diameter reflector of 101 mm (4 in.) focal length 94

12   Frequency response of cardioid microphone in
     609 mm (24 in.) diameter reflector of 178 mm
     (7 in.) focal length   95
13   Polar diagrams of a microphone in 609 mm
     (24 in.) diameter reflector of 178 mm (7 in.)
     focal length   96
14   Low-noise high-gain microphone pre-amplifier   105
15   Low-noise microphone amplifier with 125 Hz
     24 dB/octave filter   106
16   (a) Line diagram of dubbing amplifier   157
     (b) Circuit diagram of dubbing amplifier   158

Foreword

by Robert Dougall, MBE, former President
of the Royal Society for the Protection of Birds

As a boy in the twenties I well remember the excitement and interest felt throughout the nation when the BBC first broadcast the sound of the nightingale from a wood in Surrey with cello accompaniment by Beatrice Harrison. Not long afterwards Ludwig Koch became one of the best-known personalities on the wireless with his hard-won recordings of bird song.

Since those early days the study of wildlife in all its aspects has grown to be a considerable national pursuit and more and more people of all ages are finding interest and healthy recreation in the recording of sounds they hear in the field.

As equipment becomes more varied and more sophisticated the need is felt for guidance, not only for beginners but for experienced recordists as well. John Fisher, who has been Editor of the *Journal of the Wildlife Sound Recording Society* for the past eight years, has been in a position to know as well as anyone the queries and problems to be faced. He also happily has the gift of clear and simple exposition. His book will fill a considerable need and I wish it every success.

Preface

I became interested in tape recording over twenty years ago when the few portables available were expensive to buy and operate, and the resulting recording quality often left much to be desired. In consequence, for many years activities were confined to the use of a mains machine. As quality portables became available, I turned to wildlife sound recording as a change from general recording and have enjoyed the challenge ever since.

As a member of the Wildlife Sound Recording Society I served as Honorary Secretary for five years and have been Journal Editor for the last eight years. During this time I have answered many queries, particularly from those wishing to take up the hobby for the first time, and in consequence I feel I am well qualified in understanding the problems that confront the beginner and expert alike.

In this book I have tried to give guidance to the beginner and also to those with some experience who wish to develop their interest. A few technicalities have necessarily been included so that the reader will be able to choose equipment more confidently. The correct equipment is very necessary, but that does not mean it must be the most expensive. Quite modest sums spent wisely can produce much better results than unlimited resources wrongly invested. How to use this equipment in the field and final editing of tapes are dealt with as fully as is necessary to set the beginner on the right course.

I am perhaps fortunate in that I have been able to construct many of my own items of equipment for use in the field and in the studio, and a number of circuits that I have found particularly useful are included. None of these circuits are available commercially, but the amateur should have little difficulty in constructing them to his own requirements.

Chapter 2, 9 and 10 deal with many of the wildlife sounds that it is possible to record and suggest useful fields for study. Chapters 2 and 9 have been written for me by Alan Mitchell to whom I am indebted, not only for his contribution to this book but for passing on to me his enthusiasm for bird watching.

John B. Fisher
Surrey
January, 1977

Acknowledgements

The author wishes to thank John Kirby for many friendly and instructive discussions on wildlife sound recording and in particular for details of his filter and microphone pre-amplifier; Professor G. N. Patchett for permission to reproduce the results of his research into the acoustic properties of parabolic reflectors; and David Tombs for details of his microphone pre-amplifier and the results of his experiments in stereo recording.

Thanks are also due to Philips Electrical Co. Ltd for permission to publish their DNL circuit and to Mullard Ltd for their recommended circuits for amplifier and tone controls.

Photographs have kindly been provided by Uher (GB) Ltd, Hayden Laboratories Ltd, Farnell Tandberg Ltd, the 3M Co. Ltd, Ardea London, and Jack Skeel. All other photographs are by Dora Fisher.

I

The Lure of Wildlife
Sound Recording

There are many discs of wildlife sounds on the market and it is hard to name any species whose voice has not found its way onto some disc or other. A large proportion of them are produced in the form of field guides for the benefit of the vast army of bird watchers. For this purpose a brief snatch of song can be sufficient for identification. Other discs include more lengthy habitat recordings and are intended to entertain by a sound picture. All these discs have a steady sale and some people are known to make a hobby of collecting each one as it appears. In recent years a number of pre-recorded cassettes of bird song have become available. Surprisingly, the playback reproduction of many of the cassettes excels that of the majority of discs.

With all this wealth of material available one might wonder why anyone else should set out to make further recordings. Whatever the reason, more and more people are taking to the field armed with portable recorders.

In many cases interest is aroused not only by the discs and cassettes already referred to but by the various sound and television broadcasts made weekly devoted to wildlife subjects. If the listener or viewer possesses a recorder, these programmes can inspire him to try to record a dawn chorus in his own garden. Preliminary experiments of this nature may serve to convince him that recording wildlife sound presents a real challenge and he is well on the way to becoming a wildlife sound recordist.

However, most people start recording because they are already naturalists. Although they may never have used a tape recorder before, they see the device as a means of preserving sounds to be played back later, for serious study or merely to recall some particular incidents that have given them pleasure. In either case the quality of the recording is of secondary importance, the main interest being the actual programme material.

The study of recordings can lead to many discoveries. For example, as the speed of hearing response is quicker in many animals than in man, recordings can be played back at a slower speed than normal. This enables the recordist to work out how many individual notes are used in the song phrase of a particular species. It can also show why, for example, the call of one individual sandwich tern can be recognized at a great distance by its mate among a colony of maybe a thousand other members of the same species.

Many birds have an extensive repertoire. The great tit has been claimed to have at least twenty-six different calls, but what significance does each call have? We can soon differentiate between song, alarm, and contact calls, but recording the calls and noting the bird's behaviour can eventually lead to a complete understanding of the bird's language.

Another field of study is dialect. Experiments have already been conducted and prove that many birds learn at least part of their song from older birds of the same species. The song of birds that do not move about a great deal can change rapidly as the recordist travels only a short distance. Blackbirds are a typical example. In one locality the recordist finds an apparent lack of colour in the song whereas in another area all the blackbirds compete to produce the most complicated song. In the case of wrens, those in the remote Scottish islands have been separated from those on the mainland for so long that they are recognized as a sub-species and their songs reveal the difference. A full study of dialect requires the comparison of recordings made from a wide field, and the co-operation of other recordists is often vital in such work. A detailed examination may require graphical analysis using sound spectrograms involving the use of very expensive equipment, but the individual can still achieve a great deal with his relatively humble recorder.

Many of the more general naturalists simply enjoy being outdoors visiting their favourite habitats. Patiently waiting for sounds suitable to record gives them opportunities of observing many interesting activities and such recordists are seldom disappointed even if at the end of a session they have nothing recorded on tape. In exchange for their patience they at least feel refreshed by the peace and quiet away from a busy world and their knowledge of nature is constantly increasing. In the winter months they can recall these pleasant times as they listen to their recordings.

A few recordists already have considerable experience of recording in other fields and turn to recording wildlife sound as a change from their more usual activities. The quality of the recording is often far more important to such people than the actual species and they will therefore record any subject that presents itself. After a while they amass many recordings and this sometimes gratifies the instinct to collect as many different species as possible.

A small number of people take up recording to supplement their initial interest in wildlife photography and they wish to add sound tracks to cine film or to slide shows.

There is yet another class of recordist whose sole interest is the production of material calculated to win competitions. The very first wildlife sound recording competition was sponsored and organized by the BBC in 1965. The BBC's Natural History Unit at Bristol were anxious to know how many recordists existed in the British Isles and saw the competition as a useful means of establishing contact. No doubt they also hoped that the competition would produce some material for their own archives. The competition was quite successful in both respects and from the contacts established the Wildlife Sound Recording Society came into being in 1968. Thus the majority of the Society's first members were at least not opposed to the idea of competitions.

In 1968 the 3M Company introduced the first Scotch Wildlife Recording Contest and it has continued annually ever since, the number of entries also increasing with each successive year. Naturally the competition is commercially orientated with a view to promoting the sales of Scotch brand recording tape and the prizes offered are attractive. Technical perfection is now the order of the day and the winning entries must show superb composition. A straightforward, technically perfect recording of a warbler has little chance unless it is accompanied by other wildlife sounds that provide a sound stage for the principal performer. The winning entries thus nearly all appear to be chosen for their entertainment value as this is the type of recording enjoyed by the general public. At the same time the judges are on the lookout for unusual sounds – snails eating lettuce, recordings made under water, snakes, etc. – all of which have a sensation value.

In 1970, on behalf of the European Broadcasting Union, the BBC organized the first international wildlife sound recording competition as the EBU's contribution to European Conservation Year. Entries were received from all over Europe and British recordists succeeded in winning four out of the nine premier awards, including the overall winner.

The Wildlife Sound Recording Society has organized

several competitions for members and one is often arranged to find the best recording made during their annual Spring Meeting. Under these circumstances no member has any advantage in choice of habitat and it is interesting to hear the variety of recordings submitted, sometimes made under conditions when recording would not normally be attempted.

The foregoing shows the many and varied approaches to the subject. The interests of the experienced recordist change many times and few remain categorized in the manner suggested. The general recordist who turns to recording wildlife soon realizes that a knowledge of natural history is vital to his work and he often becomes a naturalist himself. The naturalist sooner or later wishes to improve the quality of his recordings, and therefore has to learn some of the more fundamental arts of pure recording.

In the ensuing chapters the equipment required and its use are described in detail, and the novice, whether a naturalist or recordist, can choose correctly and so come to operate more successfully in a rather specialized field.

Further reading

ARMSTRONG, E. A., *Discovering Bird Song*, Shire Publications Ltd, 1975.
KOCH, L., *Memoirs of a Birdman*, Phoenix House, 1955.
SIMMS, E., *Birds of the Air*, Hutchinson, 1976.
SIMMS, E., *Woodland Birds*, New Naturalist Series, Collins, 1971.

Further listening

A Salute to Ludwig Koch, BBC series 1 LP record, RED 34M.

Identifying Birds from their Sounds

by Alan Mitchell

Identifying a bird by a sound it makes is the most accurate, far-ranging and adaptable method there is in the field. There is at first, among beginners, a prejudice against using sound alone for a record of the presence of a species in the absence of a confirmatory view. It no doubt arises from the idea that bird watching is seeing birds, and that merely hearing a bird does not qualify as seeing it. The change to acceptance of sound records alone comes about partly as practice reveals the power of the discrimination of sounds and the speed and elegance of this method; partly with the realization that recording a bird requires only positive evidence of its presence by any means, not just by seeing it. The move is, one suspects, greatly encouraged by its becoming obvious that the day's list can be lacking the most interesting bird if it cannot include, for example, the unseen wader heard calling from above low cloud. There are also those moments of agony when an exciting bird eludes the watcher and disappears, leaving only the memory of its call and of the hours spent pointlessly and vandalistically trying to flush a hidden bird singing in a marsh or dense cluster of bushes. Once the call or song is regarded as a full record, making lists or censusing numbers can be done rapidly, without disturbing the habitat; and when one is freed of the necessity of seeing the bird, the call or song can be appreciated more fully.

SIGHT AND SOUND

In the field, identification will depend on clues almost invariably of sound or sight. Sound therefore has only sight with which to compete, and a closer look at our organs and senses of sight and sound makes one wonder why we trust sight records at all, never mind preferring them to sound records. The eye records a tiny, inverted image on the retina, which would be accurate enough if that was exactly what our brain received, but it is not. The image goes first to the optic centre and is processed there before arriving at the brain. Once arrived, this message is further modified, mainly by comparisons with the experience already stored in the brain, and it is interpreted in the light of this experience; and, manipulating various clues, it emerges as a personalized version of what is there. There are hosts of examples to show various aspects of the changes the scene undergoes. Optical illusions work by giving the eye misleading clues; they are most effective in distorting perspective, which is perceived entirely by clues, or by using the small, rapid movements of the eye over the scene, to confuse it. Another example is the strong and universal over-compensation for distance which makes all of us see distant hills as enormously more impressive sights than the camera shows them really to be. Then there are amateurs' drawings to show that we see what we *think* is there, not what is before our eyes. This is all too evident in those Christmas trees with down-swept branches when we can all see, if told to look, that the branches always rise, and the mistletoe berries between the leaves when they never grow there but are between the stalks lower down.

Matters are even worse if events happen unexpectedly and rapidly, as the contrary evidence of eye-witnesses to accidents bears out. The sequence of events is freely transposed as the mind re-assembles fragments of half-seen events into some order, so the sights accompanying them are transposed to match the new order. Usually, eye-witnesses to an aircraft disaster 'see' the aircraft explode in the air whilst the facts show that almost all explode only on impact. In bad light many clues may be missing, so size and speed can be interpreted as the fancy takes, but, typically, once interpreted, the version is hung on to at all costs as the absolute truth. A rapidly disappearing bird leaves only impressions and these can be juggled around before being fixed in the mind. A stone-curlew, which has prominent black and white bars along the wing, can be described as having stripes fore and aft. Even sitting birds are often described apparently carefully but quite wrongly. A grey wagtail posing well on a roof was described confidently as having bright yellow only on its back and a white underneath until, sent to have another look and told where the colour was, the observer returned admitting that the yellow was under the tail and the back was grey.

As well as over-interpretation and faulty perception, sight has the disadvantage of relying on light. Light is easily obstructed, normally travels only in straight lines, and is highly variable. Birds cannot be seen in fog, through cloud, in the dark or in dense cover, or from behind any opaque object. The colours seen depend firstly on there being enough light. The threshold for seeing colour is well above that for seeing the object. At dawn or dusk when a bird is seen it is in monochrome – shades of grey. Moonlight rarely gives enough light to see any bird, but when it does, again, there will be no colour. When the sun is near the horizon, the light it sheds is pink.

This makes white plumage appear pink and also alters the shades of other colours, so that identification by subtle colour differences is then unsafe.

The eye cannot take in the whole picture as a single piece. It scans in a series of jerks. Perhaps this is why we are so likely to miss a small part of the scene we see. Certainly most motorists will admit, if honest with themselves, that they have turned into a main road that their brain has told them quite clearly is empty of approaching traffic only to hear a squeal of brakes and tyres. In suddenly flushing a large flock of birds the eye will often miss the odd one in an otherwise uniform flock. The eye is also easily overloaded and a mixed flock of finches departing suddenly from a field of weeds may leave firm impressions of three or four species, but the observer may later find that there were six.

'Seeing is believing' maybe, but only in that we believe what we think we see and that may bear little relation to what actually happened. Illusionists live largely on their ability to exploit this failing. Training can make a great difference to the efficiency of sight. It is well known that when two people pass rapidly by an antique shop, for example, the one who is knowledgeable about antiques sees perhaps four or five objects in some detail whereas the other, if not interested, sees only the shop, if that. Those of us not aware of trees can pass every day under one of the less common species and never see it even when it is prominently in flower, whereas we will notice a laburnum in flower because we know a laburnum. Gradually, as we study birds, we see more and more and can begin to place some reliance on what we think we see.

Hearing operates differently from sight in several ways. The ear feeds the signal as straight impulses into the brain. There is less need or scope for interpretation and where it does occur it is rarely actually misleading. Are there aural illusions? In some cases incoming messages may be interpreted in the light of what the hearer believes (those who believe in ghosts hear ghosts, others hear mice, owls and contracting woodwork), but there seem to be no built-in distortions. Better still, the discrimination of sounds is incredibly precise. The ability of a listener to select one voice in a cacophony of similar voices and hear it to the effective exclusion of others is baffling. This 'cocktail party effect' works despite the fact that the complex of sounds is received reduced, like a gramophone record track, to a single wave-form and has to be reconstituted in the brain where the one series of harmonics that makes one voice distinct from others has to be selected. The selection can also be used concurrently with many others, as when we listen simultaneously to the parts followed by the trumpet, trombone and clarinet playing amongst other instruments. The conductor of an orchestra will probably be able to follow a dozen or more instrument parts at the same time. This does not mean that a good ear for music is required for learning bird calls. Some of the most skilled at this art are tone-deaf.

Sound propagates in straight lines, like light, when unobstructed, but it curves round obstacles. High-frequency sounds do this less readily than low frequencies as can be noticed when a haystack blocks the shrill call of a bird close behind it while blasting from a quarry in the same line is scarcely affected. Sound also transmits without loss through the dark and with little loss through cloud, fog and dense cover. Normal sounds can rarely be distorted in the way that daylight changes colour. Hence sound is almost inevitably heard by an observer within range, and is heard and perceived in its true form. The perception of sound seems not to suffer the upsets that plague sight when the outbreak is sudden and unexpected. The explosive call of a flushed snipe or partridge registers with clarity and precision whilst the eye is flustered and inaccurate. Neither is the ear foxed by a large mixed assemblage taking off with varying calls. The flock of finches used as an example earlier will easily be registered as six species if they call on take-off, as they usually do. Better still, with the absolute discrimination of the ear, if a flock of ten thousand redshanks flies off with a clatter of calls, if there be just one spotted redshank amongst them, the ear will unfailingly and easily pick it out, whereas the chance of its being seen is small. The obvious times when sound alone can be used, as in the dark, in fog or beside swamps and thick cover, are thus not the only circumstances in which it is greatly superior to sight, but there is another even more important advantage – the specificity of bird calls.

When a bird utters, it is communicating. Only in the unimportant case of mobbing is it communicating with a different species. All the basic sounds are designed for the ears of its own species. Songs are often used to mark territory – no bird holds territory against another species. Songs are also used for attracting mates and the very existence of species as breeding entities requires that they attract the same species – so much so that where two species are closely related and similar in appearance, it is necessary for the songs to differ strongly. The classic case is the trio of species first separated by Gilbert White through their songs, the wood warbler, willow warbler and chiffchaff. In using contact-calls when flying through the night or feeding in fog, each species is really interested in telling the others of its own species where it is, even if it will often fly with different species. Calls to indicate the finding of a source of food necessarily become specific since there is no biological gain in attracting another species to compete. The calls of nestlings are rather more general, with the advantage to the bird that they may elicit help from a passing member of another species, so these calls are not readily distinguishable by us either. For the rest of the utterances, however, the birds have done our work for us – they proclaim unambiguously what they are. Often, as in the dark or fog, the more difficult they are for us to see, the more constantly they call. The more alike in plumage they are, the more distinct the song is likely to be. This may seem to fail in a few cases. The marsh tit and willow tit are so alike that they should be separated on sight alone only after some experience in watching them after identifying them by their calls – though to a beginner the calls do not sound very different. With experience, however, the nasal 'jaaaa-jaaaa-jaaa-jaaa' or single 'jaaa' of the willow tit is instantly distinguished from the more stereotyped 'chickadee-deee-deee' of the marsh tit. The songs are quite distinct in that the marsh tit says 'duly-duly-duly' and the willow 'seeer-seeer-seeer' (although both will rarely indulge in some rich and varied warbling). The songs of tree and meadow pipits, birds very alike in plumage, differ when one knows the clicking finale of the meadow pipit and the piercing 'seeer-seeer-seeer' which ends that of the tree pipit, although they are of the same general structure and similar beginning. The calls, however, are more distinct, the meadow pipit being known by its 'sip-sip-sip' or single 'swit' whereas the tree pipit says 'tzeeng'.

Yet another advantage of sound over sight, one which is partly due to the specificity of calls and partly to inherent qualities of sound, is that (with practice, of course) a call or song gives instant, precise identification; it is very rarely ambiguous or doubtful. By contrast, the identifying by sight of many species, especially of 'critical' rare ones, depends not on just seeing the bird but on seeing the tip of the bill, colour of legs or rump, or often a part of the bird that it seldom displays when at rest, like wing-bars or outer tail feathers. A partial view may well be quite insufficient for identification whereas a partial song is usually completely diagnostic. Woodpeckers all over the world have a tone of voice which proclaims them (when vocalizing, not drumming) even to those new to the region. Species also have their particular voices.

DIFFERENT FORMS OF BIRD SONG

Bird song may be defined as modified and usually pro-longed calls used to show the bird's presence, to its mate or mates and to rival pairs or other pairs in a colony; and it is seasonal. The season may be almost all the year, as in skylark, treecreeper, goldcrest and stock-dove, but there is a short period when it is not used and the only utterances are call-notes.

It is to be expected that the songs have been, in the first place, elaborated from call-notes. The note used may be lost to its earlier purpose or it may persist. Nearly all birds have a variety of calls, and more than one may contribute to the song. In primitive songs the calls may be hardly altered from their former use, but are merely run together in some pattern.

The cuckoo has other calls than the familiar one, but during the song season it rarely uses them. The usual call is a true song, though, because it does not occur in winter quarters nor during the latter part of its stay here.

PRIMITIVE SONGS

The most primitive songs consist of but two or three notes or a string of scarcely altered call-notes with very few addi-tions. In the chiffchaff, the notes are not directly derived from the present call-note, nor are they in the cuckoo, but lapwing and oystercatcher songs are normal call-notes slightly changed only by excitement and by running them together rapidly. The song of the swift grades into the flight call, although that itself seems to be rather seasonal, so it may all be song. The long descending whickering song of the little grebe is derived from the alarm call, 'wik', and the green woodpecker's full spring-time yaffle is only an upgraded form of the 'cheff-cheff-cheff' calls. The quail's sudden, loud 'quick-quikik' and the rasping 'arp-arp' of the corncrake are distinct from any of the little-known calls of these birds. The 'tee-tee-tee-tee-tee' call of the whimbrel, heard from the night sky inland some-time in May, is used little altered as a song at the nest, while the extraordinary 'sharming' of the water rail is easily seen as an exaggerated form of one of its calls. The 'kitti-weeit, kitti-weeit' song of the common sandpiper is a minor alteration of the flight note and alarm note from which the bird has been called 'kitty-needy'.

The buntings are a group in which primitive songs abound. The yellowhammer has two usual call-notes. Often when flushed or in flight, it says 'trippi-tippit', but the casual note, also more used on longer flights, is 'chizz'. The well-known song is merely some chizzes run together at increasing speed to end usually with a 'tzeer'. The corn bunting's curious jangle is the 'tlip' call repeated until apoplexy sets in. The reed bunting has a 'tseer' call and its song is three slightly altered calls followed by a brief jangly warble. The cirl bunting has two songs, but the usual one, coming from the interior of the crown of a road-side elm, is a rapid, light 'leee-leee-leee-leee...' similar to a part of a greenfinch song. The other is almost the yellowhammer's song without the final note. Since the yellowhammer often neglects to add this note, this is not a safe way of identifying the cirl.

The songs of all the pigeons are primitive but not obviously related to any calls they may make. Other primi-tive songs are those of a single note. The bittern is one and the pheasant's crow is another. The woodcock's 'roding' song is made up of two highly disparate notes, the shrill 'tissick' followed at once by the low growling 'grrrk-grrk'. Another form of primitive song is the rapid and almost formless repetition of a single note, as in the whirring of Savi's warbler and the grasshopper warbler, and the drum-roll of the nightjar which does change from time to time in pitch by a very small amount. Sparrows sing merely by the more excited use of the 'philip' call-note. The common snipe has a mechanical song (see below) when in flight, but on the ground it uses 'chip-chop' in a sing-song, endless way. The lesser spotted woodpecker also has two songs, one of which is mechanical and the other, heard often in autumn, is 'pee-pee-pee-pee'.

PARTIALLY DEVELOPED SONGS

These are songs which are basically primitive, using a single note usually hardly changed from a regular call-note but presented with considerable variation in pitch and rhythm, or which include one or more completely different notes. They may be of very fixed pattern, largely fixed, or of indeterminate form. Examples of the first are willow warbler and chaffinch. The willow warbler's descending notes are the 'phor-weet' call-note, but they are beautifully presented in a falling cadence, dying away and then often re-starting. The chaffinch's song is its 'pink' call-note delivered briefly rising then falling and accelerating to end variously, according to the local 'dialect', but at best with a clear 'chu-weetch-oo'. The goldcrest sings a twiddling little 'widdle-dee-widdle-dee-widdle-dee...' but ends it with a sudden burst of notes which are mainly mimicked calls of other birds common in its habitat, especially the coal tit. The wood warbler has two songs, one a primitive 'seer-seer-seer' but the other a delightful clear accelerating trill, best imitated by spinning a coin on a plate. It speeds up as it falls, ending in a 'brrrr'.

The indeterminate songs in this group are typified by the nuthatch. This plainly uses at least two of its calls, 'tui' and 'pee-pee', in rapid sequences and works in hard trills and other variants not heard except in the song. The hawfinch's rather seldom heard song is similarly based on the two flight-notes 'ptik!' and 'tsseek' and is a rambling sequence of no fixed length of these notes mixed with little warblings and other notes. The crossbill performs similarly, making much use of the flight-note 'clip-clip' and twittering feeding-notes. The kingfisher uses its sharp 'ksseek' flight-note between variations and trills, and the curlew starts with its normal call then works up to the great bubbling climax. Many other waders have a similar pattern of song. In the ringed plover the flight-note 'tlui' is repeated with an accelerating and curiously rolling rhythm. The greenfinch is in this group, its full, aerial song being largely the 'ji-ji-ji' flight-note mixed with hard trills and a 'zwing-zwing-zwing'. The goldfinch, redpoll and siskin are on the borderline between this group and the next with fully developed songs, but their use of obvious call-notes places them best at the head of this group. They have songs of indeterminate length and pattern, a string of warblings and varied notes among calls. The goldfinch song is dominated by the 'twicky-wick' flight-note and that of the redpoll by the distinctive 'jidjit' flight-note but the latter also includes a long, hard roll.

The treecreeper's song, heard almost all the year, is of fixed pattern and partly of notes like its tremulous 'tseeek' call, but although developed, is brief, ending with the one distinctive feature, a rising and abruptly truncated 'sissy-swee-ip'. The pied and grey wagtails rely to some extent on their sharp calls, 'chizzick' in the pied, and a harder 'zick-zick' in the grey, but both contain a surprising richness of warbled and other notes, heard very freely also from the white wagtail, the Continental population of the pied, which is so distinct in spring.

The pipits are borderline cases, with rather fixed patterns and lengths but no obvious call-notes. The tree pipit starts, as it climbs into the air, with chaffinch-like 'chichichich', then as it tips over to descend the notes become less clear in the main falling theme, but are accompanied by a clear, piercing 'see-er, see-er, see-er'. The meadow pipit's song is altogether more tinkling and twittery and the descent tails away in a metallic whirring.

DEVELOPED SONGS

These songs have reached the stage where evident call-notes are no longer a main part of the song, if present at all, and the pattern is loose or absent. The redstart is included, despite a rather fixed pattern and a primitive start, because after the 'tree-tree-tree...' it gives a remarkable burst of rich notes, mainly mimicry of a high order and with some variation in length. The lesser whitethroat is the reverse case. It is included for its rich, varied, if subdued warbling sequence before the stereotyped 'chink-chink-chink-chink' ending by which it is so easily recognized. The wren's powerful series of trills of varying amplitude can be emitted in various lengths of a recurring pattern and are a more developed song than might appear but less so than the related dipper which warbles away even in the winter, although that song does seem to include notes like its sharp flight-note 'zixt'.

The mistle thrush has a limited range of notes, but they are of good quality and the only pattern is that they are in short phrases and these sound similar because of the lack of strikingly different notes. The song thrush is typical of birds with a song which is developed and far from simple but has not reached the higher artistry of some. The notes are clear and of great variety, but the flow is cramped by the repetition and the shortness of each phrase. A typical excerpt would be 'tu-lee-tulee-tulee, diddy-do-it, diddy-do-it, screeaagh, screeagh, victor, victor, victor...' It seems inescapable that the capercaillie's risible performance should count as a developed song. It starts to 'tick-tock' and rapidly produces a torrent of sound, then a loud 'pop, shrump-shrump!'.

The bullfinch has quite a varied little song with good

notes and heard at almost any time of year, but heard only over a short distance, for it mutters. The key phrase is a soft whistled 'twit-twit-phor-phor' which is followed by varied soft warblings and notes. The linnet might fit into the previous category but has been promoted here because of the variety of notes, tones and speed with which its twittering is uttered and its small reliance on the flight-call, 'twit-twit'. This song comes in short bursts, but they are varied, and a single song can last five or six seconds. The dunnock's song is a high-pitched warble of no set form or length, although outside the breeding season it is usually of short set length. From a moderate distance it sounds scratchy and squeaky, but at close range it is heard to include a variety of good notes. The swallow qualifies for this section because, despite its use of the flight-note 'kwinky-kwink' at the beginning, the song continues for a long, indeterminate sequence of twitters, very rich, deep notes and a hard rattled trill, and is really a good performance. The song of the house martin is similar, but with the 'trit-trit' as the flight-note and recurring through the song. It lacks a rattle but does contain rich warbling passages. The stonechat, wheatear and whinchat songs are of similar construction, shortish pretty warblings, but the whinchat can emit long passages of superb mimicry and can thus qualify as a highly developed songster. The Dartford warbler has a song similar to that of the whinchat. The key phrase is 'der-durdle-dee' and there are long, formless warblings. The rarely heard song of the red-backed shrike is a well developed if quiet and short passage of quite rich warbling.

HIGHLY DEVELOPED SONGS

These are songs which are poured out at great or moderate length, contain a multitude of rich and varied notes, and are largely free of a fixed pattern. Several of them normally contain a stream of notes mimicked from other birds.

(*Above*) The Sennheiser MKE802 electret gun microphone. This new electret form of capacitor microphone has a performance very little short of the famous Sennheiser MKH815T gun microphone at a much lower price. (*Photo:* Hayden Laboratories)
(*Below*) The author using a Sennheiser gun microphone mounted in its special windshield.

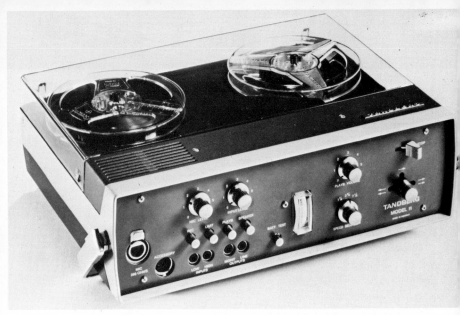

(*Above*) The Tandberg Series II, a high-quality portable recorder available only in mono form but including off-tape monitoring and many other useful features. (*Photo:* Farnell Tandberg)

(*Below*) The Nagra ISD, just one of the models in the range of high-quality portables from this well-known manufacturer. This model is two speed with off-tape monitoring. The Nagra models include a form of peak programme meter termed a 'modulometer'. (*Photo:* Hayden Laboratories)

A typical example is that of the garden warbler. This is a long warbling containing some deep and throaty notes and other high, clear notes, rambling on but well delivered. At the beginning of the season the blackcap's song is similar to that of the garden warbler but lacks the deep notes and contains more whistling. Towards the end of the season, and for a brief period, the blackcap breaks through to a loud high-whistled ending at the height of its song. This has a pattern, but although easily recognized and usually falling to an end something like 'wheety-whoo', it has details individual to each bird and can vary considerably. The blackbird is more typical, having no pattern beyond being delivered in short groups of phrases, and contains a great variety of highly individual phrases. Some birds develop passages of five or six notes in true musical intervals and can chance upon a known tune. Laurel and Hardy's signature tune 'Cuckoo' can sometimes be heard perfectly rendered. Some birds use more mewing notes and most have a recognizable phrase or two of their own.

The whitethroat, at its best period only, emits long streams of warbling, scratchy in parts but containing many good notes and some occasional mimicry. The sedge warbler has an indefinite length of song, with some mimicry and varied passages, marred only by the constant appearance of the scold-note 'tuktuk', and delivered at great speed. The reed warbler song is of the same form but is delivered with a steady, measured rhythm, and a softer 'churruck' replaces the hard scold. There is more mimicry, too, with tree sparrow, reed bunting and linnet frequently quoted. The great reed warbler has a similarly measured song with a beat, but it is shorter, far more powerful and contains a loud croaking 'grrk-grrk' and also bursts of pure loud notes. One ended every burst of song by rising to a crescendo with a splendid 'peeloo-peeloo-peeloo' when it sang throughout the Whitsun bank holiday at Frensham Great Pond amidst paddling children. The marsh warbler, however, has the highest developed song amongst these warblers. This stream of loud, clear warbling is one long recital of other birds' calls and songs connected by rich warbling. In a single burst of song a good performer may use the notes of swallow, house martin, greenfinch, linnet, goldfinch and little owl several times each.

The woodlark song is clearly among the best few in this top group. It can extend for twenty minutes or more, especially on a warm, clear moonlit night, and pours down from the sky in an endless flow of falling sequences of clear, silvery notes as the bird circles several hundred feet up in the sky. Each phrase starts anew, rising for a few notes then tumbling down, often ending with the liquid 'lululululu' note from which the bird has been called 'lulu' and which appears in its generic name, *Lullula*. There can be no doubt of the quality of the woodlark song, but that of the skylark only doubtfully qualifies in this group. Much better known and hence generally highly rated, this song can be twenty minutes long, although it is usually less than five minutes; and, like the woodlark's, it can be heard from the first sunny day in January, though not at night. It has, however, a mechanical quality, a rather poorly differentiated whirring almost hiding the clearer notes and mimicry. Skylarks near saltings frequently use the notes of ringed plover and redshank in their songs.

Using the criteria here adopted, the starling's performance comes into this group, surprising as it may be. It is rambling, contains mimicry and is a highly individual affair. Nearly all town starlings repeatedly use the pied wagtail's flight-call, 'chizzick', the moorhen's explosive 'cherrook!' and a poor effort at the lesser spotted woodpecker's 'pee-pee-pee' song. Many birds, however, add their own variations and include local sounds in their repertoire. The rest of it is a strange mixture of whizzles, crackling sounds, clicks and clear whistles, unmusical to us, but varied and rather fun. The robin is a fine songster, and there are two forms of song. In the autumn, male and female take up different and competing territories and both defend and define their territories by song, but of a different kind from the spring song. Cock and hen now sing with a strange, wistful quality that goes so well with woodsmoke in a misty autumn dusk. On what sounds like indrawn breath, the first phrase is a liquid patter of notes leading to some long-drawn thin notes and then often a cascade of fuller ones falling over each other.

At the very top of the list of accomplished singers, the nightingale stands supreme. Many bird watchers and others profess to admire the blackbird's song more and prefer it to that of the nightingale, but this seems to be confusing nostalgia for late spring evenings in the garden with the quality of song. The nightingale's song excels in every aspect except one. Although of undefined duration, it is made up from a limited number of phrases and these are not varied greatly by individuals. After conceding that, however, all is in the superlative. No other bird in Europe, and few in the world, shows such a range of power, pitch and timing, and all in rapid succession. The strong notes can easily be heard half a mile away (helped at night by the surrounding quiet, but audible from nearly as far through the chorus of other birds by day) yet the notes following may seem very quiet, although still carrying well. The 'jug-jug' note must be the deepest-pitched song note after the bittern's boom, but the keening note that often follows seems to hover on the upper threshold of our hearing.

Many phrases are thrown out at great speed, but the keening note is slowed down and drawn out, only to give way to a sudden, upsweeping burst of rich, deep notes.

MECHANICAL SONGS

Among our birds, the three woodpecker species and the snipe use non-vocal means to make their song or one of their two songs (in the lesser spotted woodpecker and the snipe). The woodpeckers beat their bills against trees or posts, or rarely roofs, to make the drumming songs. The great spotted makes a loud, ringing drum with a sharp beginning and rapidly fades away. It can usually be heard in late January, increasing to a peak in early May and then stopping. The lesser spotted makes a soft drumming that starts as it continues, evenly and for noticeably longer than that of the great spotted. It starts in February, reaches a great peak for only a few days in April and then ceases but recurs spasmodically from August to November.

The green woodpecker is widely believed not to drum at all. However, a microphone recording on to tape was left running at dawn in a Hampshire forest by R. Genever, living in a caravan, and the tape has the calls of a green woodpecker working around very close to the microphone. Between the calls are periods of a deep, slow, rolling drumming utterly distinct from that of the other woodpeckers. It must be a very rare occurrence.

The snipe has its own way of making a second song. It towers in the dusk or dawn sky until it is some three hundred feet up, then side-slips downwards at great speed with its tail spread. The two outermost feathers stand clear of the others and buzz, while the wings, beating fast, modulate the current of air through them giving a whinnying effect. The resulting buzzing 'wahwahwah...' is very like the bleat of a goat.

MIMICRY

Mimicry is very much more widespread among our birds than is generally realized. The starling's efforts are well known, but few people seem to have noticed the more accurate use of other birds' calls at the end of the goldcrest's little song. There are one or two at the end of nearly every song, usually of great, blue, coal or marsh tit. A chaffinch will occasionally add the 'tchik!' of a great spotted woodpecker to the end of every song; apparently this is more frequent on the Continent.

As mentioned above, some redstarts are superb mimics, adding two or three quotes to the end of most songs. One talented bird used calls from seventeen species. A good whinchat had a repertoire of over twenty calls and songs, all very truly reproduced. The song thrush often uses the 'tui-tui-tui' of the nuthatch as one phrase in its song while the robin is mischievous and ends its song with the key phrase of the blackcap only in the first few weeks in April when one is hoping to hear the real thing. The garden warbler is even more trying when among its infrequently used small store of mimicked calls it also ends with the blackcap's phrase. The skylark and the sedge, reed and marsh warblers have been mentioned for their mimicry.

Some birds use mimicry only or mainly in their sub-song. This is a sort of mumbling song-practice which most birds do from time to time and is not sung from a prominent perch nor declaimed to all. It is done quietly, from the centre of thick cover usually, and when the bird is either feeding or just sitting still. The great exponent of this is the jay, perhaps because it has no true full song. Occasionally one sits in a bush and pours out a stream of mixed notes in a very pleasant warble, but the odd aberrant noise like a perfect bleat of a sheep or greenfinch trill makes it apparent that it is not all random notes.

This is probably the most valuable field for the recordist. There is no way other than a good tape-record to convince others of the validity of some claims of mimicry. The most striking cases are the whitethroats. Both lesser and common have been heard by the writer singing a stream of sub-song. Listening to them without suspecting mimicry he was brought up sharply by the churr of mistle thrush unmistakably rendered. Listening harder, it was then apparent that much of the babble was in fact mimicry, but given at such an unnaturally high speed that until this was noticed it seemed random noise. There were then no tape recorders and the record of the mimicry of numerous other birds' calls by these whitethroats was not acceptable.

It is very probable that taping the sub-songs of many species would reveal a wealth of mimicry. The jay's performances are sure to be full of it. Furthermore, the full songs of many species not at present regarded as mimics will surely be shown to contain examples. Since the redstart and whinchat are such masters of the art, attention should be paid to the songs of wheatear and stonechat, whilst dunnock and dipper, garden warbler, pied wagtail, white wagtail, goldfinch and swallow all have the form of song in which much mimicry could be hidden.

3

Microphones

INTRODUCTION

The microphone is a device used to convert sound pressure waves into electric signals. In any audio equipment, whether it be a pick-up, loudspeaker or microphone, the faithful transduction of physical pressures into electrical signals and vice versa is recognized as being a very difficult process, and these are always the weakest links in any audio system.

In the case of recording, the microphone is the first link in the chain of events and any distortion at this stage can never be corrected. It is, therefore, not surprising that the experienced recordist gives the choice of microphone for any given purpose very serious consideration.

In the past many methods have been devised to convert sound pressures into electrical signals, with varying degrees of success. Some of these methods have survived to the present day and new methods have been added. A microphone for use by a wildlife sound recordist must be robust, capable of being handled and suitable for use outdoors in all kinds of weather. These requirements restrict the methods used to two types, namely the moving coil (often called dynamic) and the capacitor (sometimes called electrostatic). All the other types are of academic interest and will not be described.

MOVING COIL AND CAPACITOR MICROPHONES

As its name implies, the moving coil basically consists of a coil of thin wire elastically suspended between the poles of a powerful permanent magnet. A diaphragm is connected to the coil so that when sound pressures are applied to the diaphragm the coil is caused to have a slight movement. This movement is sufficient to cause a small current to be generated in the coil. The action is similar to that of most loudspeakers, which of course operate in the reverse manner, i.e. a current from the amplifier is passed through the coil which moves as a result of its being suspended in a strong magnetic field. In this case the coil is attached to the cone of the loudspeaker and the cone generates sound pressures. A loudspeaker may, in fact, be used in reverse as a microphone, although this can hardly be recommended as a regular practice.

The capacitor microphone consists of a metallized diaphragm opposite a metal plate thus forming an air spaced capacitor. Movement of the diaphragm as a result of sound pressure waves causes minute variations in the value of the capacitor. One pole of the capacitor must be polarized so that a current can flow through the capacitor in proportion to the varying capacitance. The output of the capacitance is minute and must be immediately amplified to bring it up to a useful value, and the body of the microphone contains the necessary pre-amplifier.

In some designs the body of the microphone carries a battery for powering the built-in amplifier, in others a separate external battery has to be used. In such cases the recorder's own battery can be arranged to supply the power.

With the normal capacitor microphone, the battery used for the built-in amplifier is also used to polarize the microphone, but a more recent development is to make the diaphragm of permanently charged material. This gives rise to the new name 'electret capacitor microphone', often simply reduced to 'electret'. In its simplest form the electret is quite cheap, and many cassette recorders are now being produced with a built-in electret microphone. More advanced forms of electret have a performance not far short of the normal capacitor microphone, and as they are not as costly it is safe to prophesy that this type will gain in popularity.

Any form of capacitor microphone is more complicated than the moving coil pattern, and inevitably is more costly. A cheap capacitor microphone will not give nearly such good results as a moving coil microphone of the same price, but a good capacitor microphone surpasses the performance of a moving coil microphone in nearly all respects. This is not, however, a condemnation of the moving coil microphone, the best of which give a very good account of themselves.

MICROPHONE SPECIFICATION

Before a microphone can be chosen for any particular application its full specification must be studied. Fortunately, the better manufacturers make these specifications available, but if none is available it is better to ignore the product completely. The purchaser is nowadays protected by the Trade Descriptions Act and those manufacturers who refuse to publish a full specification may well be wishing to conceal the truth.

The full specification is not easy to understand, and many users who have no desire to delve more deeply can often be satisfied with simple guide-lines indicating that, in the manufacturer's view, model X in his range is suitable for studio work, model Y for music, model Z for amateur recording and so on. Model Z may well appear suitable for the amateur purely because of its cost, but it may be completely unsatisfactory for wildlife sound recording.

Thus the wildlife sound recordist must have a deeper knowledge of how to interpret specifications, and although his choice may be limited by cost, at least he will know the limitations set by finance.

From the specification title we will first learn the method of operation and having thus assured ourselves that the method is moving coil or capacitor and hence that the general method used is suitable for our application, we can then delve more deeply into the other characteristics of frequency response, sensitivity, etc.

FREQUENCY RESPONSE

Frequency response is of prime importance as one cannot hope to record the full song of a bird unless the microphone produces some electrical output for all the audible frequencies used in the bird song. However, this alone is not sufficient if we are hoping to reproduce the sounds faithfully. We need to be assured that each note will be reproduced at its correct level respective to all the other notes.

Thus a microphone with a response simply stated as being from 40 Hz to 12 000 Hz will produce some electrical output when subjected to sound pressures between these limits, and if the bird's song is contained within these limits, a signal will be available for recording over the complete repertoire. Assuming for the moment that these signals can be faithfully recorded and played back, the reproduction will bear a distinct resemblance to the original, but our ears might well tell us that something is not quite right.

Thus we need to know just how the electrical output varies between the limits of response, and this is shown on the frequency response curve. A typical curve is shown in

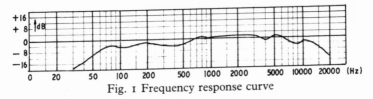

Fig. 1 Frequency response curve

Fig. 1. It will be noted that the vertical curve is shown in decibels and that the horizontal frequency scale is logarithmic.

The novice often experiences some difficulty in understanding the term 'decibel', and as the term is frequently used in this and ensuing chapters, a few words of explanation are appropriate.

The term was first used by the American inventor, Alexander Graham Bell, who noticed that the response of the human ear was non-linear. In other words, he found that it required a tenfold increase in signal power for the listener to judge that the sound had doubled in intensity. He therefore termed this increase one bel. Thus two bels represents a hundredfold increase in power, three bels a thousandfold, minus one bel a reduction to one-tenth and so on. The bel, therefore, is not a quantity but a ratio of power, in fact a common logarithmic ratio.

A tenfold increase or decrease is rather a large amount, so the bel was subdivided into ten equal parts called decibels; although ten decibels means a tenfold increase, because the ratio is logarithmic we must not make the simple error of assuming that a decibel increase means doubling the power.

The terms bel and decibel are correctly abbreviated to B and dB after the inventor's name but it has also become common practice to write db.

Electrical power is measured in watts, but provided the load impedance remains unaltered, the power is proportional to the square of the voltage. Accordingly if we wish to compare voltages instead of power, then the increase in dB must be doubled. For this reason the suffix V or W (alternatively 'm' standing for milliwatts) is often added to dB to make it clear whether voltages or watts have been compared. It is also important to quote a reference level. For example, to say that Jack has twice as many apples as Jill does not tell you how many apples Jack has until you are told that Jill has two.

Returning now to the frequency response curve shown in Fig. 1, as we are more interested in how the output varies relative to the frequency than in knowing its precise value, the use of the decibel notation becomes clear.

If the curve were a horizontal straight line extending from 1 Hz to 20 000 Hz, few would dispute that we would have a perfect microphone so far as frequency response was concerned.

The human ear can scarcely detect a change of less than 3 dB so that provided the curve keeps within a limit of ± 3 dB and extends at both ends to cover the frequencies known to exist from the sound source, the instrument will be completely adequate. This assumes for the moment that the reproducing channel and the listener's ears are also capable of dealing with the sound. A young person's ears detect frequencies up to about 16 000 Hz but by middle age this is reduced to about 12 000 Hz. Recording sounds and reproducing them up to 16 000 Hz is quite demanding on equipment and the recordist must make up his mind as to how far he proposes to go in this direction. There is little doubt that elements of many bird songs extend very high, even beyond 16 000 Hz, but whether it is worthwhile to try to record these frequencies for anything but scientific purposes must be left to the reader to decide.

At the lower frequencies, very few wildlife species, especially birds, produce much sound, but as most mechanical interference usually occurs in this range, many recordists purposely introduce a bass cut filter either during recording or later during copying. Alternatively, microphones designed to have a decreasing bass response can often help. This is referred to as a bass roll-off feature.

If the microphone is to be used almost exclusively in a reflector, consideration must be given to the effect the reflector has on the response of the open microphone. This is explained more fully in Chapter 5.

The frequency response of the recorder must not be overlooked as it is a complete waste of money to invest in a microphone whose performance cannot be realized. On the other hand, microphones supplied 'free' with a recorder seldom have as good a response as the recorder and a better microphone is usually required to secure the best performance of which the recorder is capable.

Microphones of the two types suitable for wildlife sound recording purposes can be purchased having very adequate frequency response characteristics, those having the smoothest and most extended response being the more expensive. In general, capacitor microphones have better frequency response curves than their dynamic counterparts but are even more expensive and have certain other drawbacks. Cheap capacitor microphones can often lead to disappointing results compared with a similar investment in a dynamic microphone.

The response curve in Fig. 1 refers to a reasonably good-quality dynamic microphone and would be more than adequate for all kinds of wildlife sound recording. This is not to say that microphones with an inferior response cannot be used to produce quite satisfactory recordings.

SENSITIVITY AND NOISE

These terms are fairly self explanatory but their importance, particularly in wildlife sound recording, is not nearly so well appreciated.

Sensitivity is defined as the electrical output for a specified air pressure acting on the diaphragm of the microphone. The actual air pressure depends on the magnitude of the sound generated at its source and its distance away, reducing in accordance with the inverse square law. The sounds from wildlife are often weaker and farther away than sounds encountered in other forms of recording, so it is essential to use a microphone that has a good sensitivity.

If microphones of comparatively low sensitivity are used the signal will have to be amplified more than normal and the noise level relative to the signal will become unacceptable. 'Noise' is a form of self-generated random signal present in all electrical circuits and is caused by the thermal movement of electrons in the various components. The noise is generally constant but it is its size relative to the wanted signal that is so important if it is to be unnoticed.

The methods used by manufacturers to specify sensitivity vary considerably, making comparison complicated. The electrical output is expressed either in milliwatts or in millivolts, but a whole host of units are in use for expressing pressure. To further complicate matters the output may be expressed in decibel notation with numerous zero reference levels. Pressure is a measure of force applied to a specific area, and in one system based on centimetres and grams the unit of pressure is called the dyne per square centimetre. Using a more modern method based on metres and kilograms, the unit is called the newton per square metre. As the units of mass and length are directly related, the units of pressure are also related; thus 1 newton per square metre is exactly 10 dynes per square centimetre.

In some countries an additional unit called the pascal has been adopted for the newton per square metre. In many industrial applications the newton per square metre is too small a unit, so the bar, comprising 10^5 newtons per square metre, has been adopted, one bar approximating to normal atmospheric pressure. In audio work the bar is too large a unit, so microbars are used.

Manufacturers use all these systems, so the following equations will prove useful in making comparisons.

$$1 \text{ N/sq. m} = 1 \text{ Pa} = 10\mu\text{b} = 10 \text{ dynes/sq. cm}$$

The sensitivity will be specified at one particular frequency, usually 1000 Hz, as, of course, its output will vary with frequency in accordance with the response curve.

With all this information we can compare the performance of different makes of microphone. For example, one very popular make is quoted as having an output of −75 dB below 1 volt/dyne/square centimetre. Another popular microphone having the same impedance is quoted as having an output of 2.4 mV/Pa. Table 1 gives the voltages represented by a number of dB ratios based on a reference level of 1 volt. From this table it will be noted that the first microphone has an output of 0.18 volts/dyne/sq. cm, and as we know that one dyne per sq. cm is one tenth of a pascal, we immediately see that while the first microphone would produce 0.18 millivolts the second microphone would produce 0.24 millivolts in exactly the same circumstances, leading us to the conclusion that the second microphone is $33\frac{1}{3}$ per cent more sensitive and, all other items being equal, the second microphone would be chosen.

In general, dynamic microphones with a good frequency response tend to be less sensitive, but there are exceptions. In the comparison above, the second microphone actually possesses a better frequency response curve than the first. A third microphone from the same stable as the second microphone, however, has an even better frequency response, but its sensitivity is only 1.3 mV/Pa, and while either of the first two microphones will produce very acceptable results, the third is likely to be disappointing.

Table 1

dBV table	OdB = 1 V
−60	1.00 mV
−70	0.32
−71	0.28
−72	0.25
−73	0.23
−74	0.20
−75	0.18
−76	0.16
−77	0.14
−80	0.10
−83	0.07

$$dB = 20 \log \frac{V1}{V2}$$

Comparisons between the sensitivities of dynamic and capacitor microphones show that the latter type is much more sensitive, and at first sight this may be thought to be a big advantage. However, it must be remembered that the higher output is the direct result of the built-in pre-amplifier and this can be a source of noise.

The absolute measurement of noise is possible and is sometimes quoted, but often it is related as a dB ratio to the normal signal usually expected. One way is to relate it to the strength of signal derived from a microphone at peak levels of human speech when the speaker would be holding the microphone. A similar level of sound would be received by the microphone when placed before a group of musicians. This strength of signal is rarely encountered in wildlife sound recording, and even if the signal were only half as strong, the noise relative to the signal would immediately be doubled.

The noise generated by a dynamic microphone is caused by the coil and its connections and is generally very low. Provided the signal is not subject to gross amplification, the noise will be unnoticeable. The degree of amplification used will depend on the strength of signal and the sensitivity of the microphone. In wildlife sound recording there is a limit to the strength of signal governed by the difficulty of approach without causing disturbance.

The noise generated by a capacitor microphone is generated in the microphone's own pre-amplifier. Great care is taken in designing such amplifiers which usually include field effect transistors. Such transistors do not use as many resistors in their operating circuits and it is usually the resistors which are guilty of generating the most noise. However, even with care, the signal-to-noise ratio is often not as good as that of a much cheaper dynamic microphone. As the sensitivity is generally much higher than that of a dynamic microphone, the temptation to use them at a greater distance is strong, but this can lead to an even worse signal-to-noise ratio.

IMPEDANCE

It should be noted that the typical sensitivities quoted above were for microphones of 200 ohm impedance.

The impedance of a dynamic microphone is fixed by the impedance of the coil and its connections, and as it will vary with frequency, the specification usually quotes the value at one given frequency, often 1000 Hz.

The impedance of any microphone is often generally referred to as being high, medium or low, typical figures being 50 000, 200 and 25 ohms respectively. The coil of a dynamic microphone is designed in conjunction with the magnetic system to produce the desired sensitivity and frequency response and usually results in the microphone being medium or low impedance. To convert to high impedance a transformer is incorporated in the body of the microphone which converts the impedance in the ratio of the square of the turns on the primary and the secondary. Thus if the coil has a 200 ohm impedance and the transformer has a ratio of 1:10 the effective output impedance would be 20000 ohms. On some models, when a transformer is incorporated a switch is included so that the transformer can be bypassed and the microphone can then be used as either a low or high impedance model.

The impedance of a capacitor microphone is a measurement of the output characteristics of the built-in preamplifier and for any such circuit there is an output impedance as well as a source impedance. Both are quoted, but it is the output or load impedance which is the more important when considering matching.

Thus many models of dynamic microphone are available in several impedance versions and the purchaser must specify on his order which version he requires. The usual method of selection is to relate it to the input impedance of the recorder with which it is intended to use the microphone the most. An exact match is not vital but a complate mismatch can result in there being no transfer of signal at all or at best a considerable loss of signal.

A 200 to 300 ohm microphone would efficiently transfer its signal when directly connected to a recorder having an input impedance of up to 1000 ohm, and a 20000 ohm microphone would work into about 70000 ohm input. But a 300 ohm microphone will produce little into 70000 ohm and 20000 ohm would never produce a signal in a 1000 ohm input.

Most recorders have an input impedance of around 200 to 1000 ohm but sometimes higher input impedances are used. However, before a high impedance microphone is specified, consideration should be given to using a microphone impedance matching transformer.

DIRECTIONAL CHARACTERISTICS

A microphone that is equally sensitive to sounds from all directions is termed omni-directional. In practice, sounds from the rear are partially masked by the body of the microphone. Microphones designed to be more receptive to sounds from a single direction are termed uni-directional. The sensitivity of such a microphone can be plotted on a polar diagram as shown in Fig. 2, showing that the microphone is least sensitive to sounds approaching from the rear. The general shape of such polar diagrams is heart shaped, or cardioid, and gives this type of microphone its characteristic name.

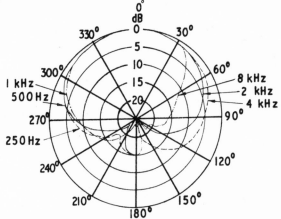

Fig. 2 Polar diagram

Thus the main point to note about cardioid microphones is that they have a maximum sensitivity to sound waves approaching the front of the microphone while the sensitivity to other sound waves falls off progressively as the sound waves impinge on the side until at the rear the microphone is practically dead. The degree to which this sensitivity falls off determines whether the microphone may be called super-cardioid and in the extreme super-hyper-cardioid. Microphones in the latter category are thus extremely directional and are commonly referred to as gun microphones because in order to achieve the characteristic, the body is so elongated that it appears to form the barrel of a gun. Such microphones have to be pointed fairly accurately at the subject to be recorded so that the maximum output signal is generated.

Both dynamic and capacitor microphones are available in omni and cardioid forms and the wildlife sound recordist makes use of nearly all of them from time to time, depending on the particular field technique being employed. This is explained more fully in Chapter 7.

Both forms of microphone may be mounted in a reflector, except the gun microphone which is a special case. The high sensitivity of the capacitor gun microphone makes it suitable for hand holding, and it is often used instead of the more familiar reflector. Gun microphones of the dynamic pattern can rarely be hand-held close enough to the subject, and as they must always be aimed with some accuracy at the subject, it is not always practical to use them at the end of unattended leads. Such microphones have, therefore, a rather limited use and cannot be recommended.

SHAPE AND WEIGHT, ETC.

The specification includes a lot more easily-understood information relating to shape, size, weight and terminal arrangements, and each piece of information has some importance depending on the application.

The shape is important in considering how the microphone shall be mounted in a reflector and how efficiently it can be shielded from the wind. The weight is a consideration when it has to be added to that of a reflector and held aloft for lengthy periods of time.

Nowadays most microphones are manufactured in stick form and this is a convenient shape for mounting in a reflector, hand holding or supporting on a stand. Some include a rather bulbous end which may be claimed to act as a windshield; but, as will be seen when considering the effect of mounting the microphone in a reflector, it may actually serve to curtail its upper frequency response. In any case such devices are seldom of much value as a true windshield.

The weight of a dynamic microphone usually exceeds that of a capacitor microphone, as permanent magnets to produce good results must be substantial.

The construction of the body itself has a bearing on shielding from stray fields and handling noise. As most handling noise produces low-frequency sounds, a microphone with a good bass response can be more susceptible to handling noise than a model inferior in this respect. If the subjects to be recorded do not include bass frequencies in their repertoire, a microphone with a diminished bass response will not only capture the full repertoire, but will not be anything like so susceptible to handling noise. But, in any case, mounts incorporating resilience can offset most handling noise.

Finally there are the lead connections. Some cheaper forms of microphone are supplied with a captive lead to the end of which the purchaser must attach his own plug, but all the better ones end with a socket suitable for one of a variety of connecting plugs. Popular versions include DIN and XLR.

MICROPHONES FOR STEREO RECORDING

For recording in stereo it is usually accepted that at least two microphones are used, and, needless to say, they must be of the same pattern. Further, individual characteristics should match as closely as possible, and some manufacturers even offer specially matched pairs. Unfortunately, the general types offered in matched pairs may not be suitable for our purpose; for example, their sensitivities may be too low. However, every good microphone is supplied with its individual response curve showing that the microphone's performance complies with its general specification. Most stockists are prepared to select a pair with closely matching curves.

WINDSHIELDS AND RESILIENT MOUNTINGS

Wind is one of the biggest problems encountered by the wildlife sound recordist in the field. Even a slight breeze on an unprotected microphone is sufficient to ruin the recording, so it is essential that an efficient windshield should be fitted and used at all times.

When the microphone is mounted in a reflector a quite efficient and cheap windshield can easily be made, as described in Chapter 5, but an efficient shield for an open-type microphone is not easy to produce.

Most microphone manufacturers list windshields for each of their models and these usually take the form of a moulded foam sleeve that simply slides over the end of the microphone. These are effective in reducing the blasting caused by the breath of a person speaking directly into the microphone, but there is still some noise, albeit very little, in comparison with the strength of the signal. Typical wildlife sounds produce a much worse signal-to-noise ratio and the degree of wind protection afforded by such devices is generally insufficient.

For our purpose experiments indicate that the best wind protection is achieved when there is a free air space between the foam and the microphone. This is endorsed by at least two makes of windshield specially designed for use in conjunction with gun microphones. These comprise a moulded plastic open mesh tube approximately 150 mm in diameter and lined with a fine woven material. As the microphone is only about 25 mm in diameter there is a free air space of more than 60 mm between the shield and the microphone. Such windshields are expensive and are not made for more conventional-sized microphones, but smaller versions can be made by the handyman employing suitable tin cans to form the ends, expanded aluminium for the cylinder, and acoustic foam as lining.

If the microphone is to be hand-held some form of resilient mounting is highly desirable. The windshield for the gun microphone just described incorporates a resilient mount, the clips being mounted within the tube via flexible rubber pillars. In a home-made version the microphone can be suspended between rubber bands supported on screwed rods which are also used to retain the end caps of the cylinder.

For stereo recording the two microphones may be mounted in a split reflector and the same form of wind protection can be used as with any other reflector. If gun microphones or any other forms of open microphone are to be used, each can be shielded as described above, but as microphones for stereo cannot be moved during use, there is not the same need for resilient mounting. Much success has been obtained by mounting the two microphones in a drum about 300 mm diameter and 250 mm deep. The top and bottom can be made of 10 mm plywood and spaced apart by metal rods which also support the acoustic foam side. The microphones are held by clips fixed to a vertical rod located in the centre.

MICROPHONE LEADS AND CONNECTIONS

Although a great deal of recording is done with the microphone near the recorder, there are many times when it is necessary to increase the length of the microphone leads and this can cause many problems including loss of high frequencies, radio interference and hum. The microphone current is so small that resistive loss is negligible but the capacitive effect on the high frequencies can be disastrous.

The longer the microphone leads the greater will be the electrical capacity between the conductors. Now the capacitive reactance X is inversely proportional to the capacitance C and the frequency of the signal f. Thus:

$$X = \frac{1}{Cf}$$

This reactance virtually shunts the recorder input and it will be noted that the greater the capacitance and the higher the frequency, the lower the reactance becomes. If this reactance is very much lower than the input impedance of the recorder, the microphone current will tend to bypass the recorder completely and the effect is progressively worse as the frequency increases. Accordingly, if the high frequencies are not to be severely attenuated, the input impedance at the recorder end of the microphone cable must be kept low.

In practice this can be achieved by using recorders having low or medium input impedances and microphones of matching impedance. However, if a recorder is chosen having a high input impedance, there are a number of alternatives available (see Fig. 3). For recording with short leads a high impedance microphone can be directly coupled to the recorder – Fig. 3(a). The same microphone may be used with long leads, but a matching transformer is then required at each end of the cable so that the cable operates at low impedance – Fig. 3(b). Finally, a low or medium impedance microphone may be used with one matching transformer at the recorder end – Fig. 3(c). As matching transformers are much cheaper than good microphones, probably the cheapest method is the last, but this has the drawback that the matching transformer must be used even when using short leads and it is an extra item to carry.

Further problems arise from using long leads, namely

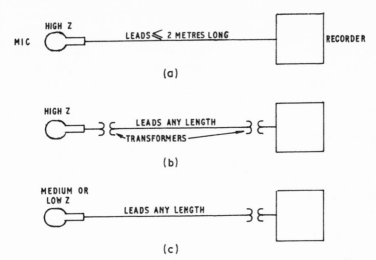

Fig. 3 Matching microphones to a high input impedance recorder
with long microphone leads

hum and radio interference. The longer the leads the more
chance there is that hum will be induced from some stray
magnetic field, and the leads can also act as an efficient
radio aerial which, with the coil of a microphone, can
easily present a tuned circuit. The high gain of the recorder
does the rest and we are in the unhappy position of
having a radio receiver in our hands when we want to
record a completely different set of signals.

There are two kinds of microphone cable, one consisting
of a single core surrounded by a screen similar to the
familiar co-axial leads used for TV aerials and the other
consisting of two cores surrounded by a screen.

The single-core cable uses the screen as one of the conductors and at the same time connects the body of the
microphone to the chassis of the recorder. This is known
as unbalanced line working and is shown in Fig. 4(a). Unbalanced line working can also be achieved using twin-core
screened cable as in Fig. 4(b). Any induced hum tends
to be restricted to the screen and should not affect the

signal. The best method is to use balanced line working as shown in Fig. 4(c). This implies that the recorder is equipped with a balanced microphone input. In theory any signal is induced equally in the same direction in each core and these cancel out in the input transformer, whereas the unwanted signal, being in an opposite direction in the two cores, is not affected.

If the recorder is not equipped with a balanced microphone input, the method shown in Fig. 4(b) must be used; alternatively, an external transformer can be used. A microphone pre-amp, described in Chapter 6, having a balanced input, could also be used feeding into the line input of the recorder.

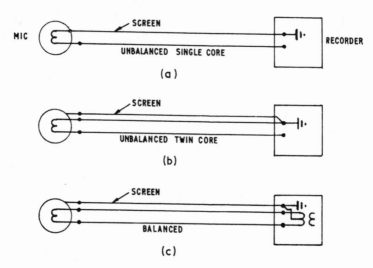

Fig. 4 Balanced and unbalanced microphone connections

4

The Tape Recorder

INTRODUCTION

The first recording of an animal was made by Ludwig Koch, who as a small boy captured the sounds of a bird on an Edison phonograph. This machine recorded sounds on a wax cylinder using purely mechanical means. The transition through wax disc recording to the modern tape recorder is largely a matter of history.

The principle of magnetic recording was suggested long before Ludwig Koch made his first recording but at that time there was no means of amplifying the minute signals involved. The thermionic valve took care of this and the first attempts to produce wire recorders were made shortly before the Second World War. During the war years a lot of development took place in Germany so that shortly afterwards domestic tape recorders began to appear and all professional recordings were made on tape. The arrival of the transistor more than twenty-five years ago heralded the era of portable recording. Since then hundreds of different models of reel-to-reel portables have appeared, only to disappear as compact cassette portables arrived.

The success of the cassette system since its first introduction by Philips has been phenomenal. A new generation of tapes incorporating non-ferric oxide have appeared, together with many noise reduction systems, resulting in a quality not far short of that produced by the best disc-playing equipment. In spite of the fact that pre-recorded cassettes are more costly than their disc equivalents, a very wide range of material is available from which one can only conclude that the ease of use more than makes up for slightly inferior quality.

The endless loop cartridge is a further development aimed at 'in car' entertainment for which machines are available that are even easier to operate than the compact cassette. Such machines, however, are hardly suitable for the creative recordist.

Whether the machine chosen for wildlife sound recording is reel-to-reel or cassette, the general principles of operation are the same and a working knowledge will be found invaluable in understanding the specification and facilities offered by any particular model.

BASIC COMPONENTS OF A RECORDER

A complete recorder comprises a tape transport, a pre-amplifier, a power amplifier and a loudspeaker. Such a machine is capable of recording and replaying over its own loudspeaker; alternatively, an external speaker may be used. If the power amplifier and loudspeaker are omitted, the machine is termed a tape deck and can record; but to replay, an external amplifier and loudspeaker must be used.

TAPE TRANSPORT

The tape transport system is the means by which the tape is drawn over the electromagnets, which are referred to as heads. It is, of course, essential that the tape passes over the heads at exactly the correct speed and that this speed is maintained as constant as possible. Any variation in the speed will result in a wavering quality in the sounds recorded. Technically, the speed variation is termed 'wow' and 'flutter'. 'Wow' is the result of slow cyclic speed changes whereas 'flutter' is caused by very rapid irregular speed changes. Where one ends and the other begins is somewhat indeterminate but the aggregate is expressed as a percentage variation from the desired fixed speed. The audible effects of wow and flutter depend on the type of sounds being recorded and are most noticeable on pro- gramme material containing sustained notes such as church bells or the slow movement of a piano concerto. For these sounds the percentage wow and flutter content must not exceed 0.15 per cent. For speech or music con- sisting of brief staccato notes, very often encountered in pop music, a wow and flutter content of 0.2 per cent or even greater might not be detectable. For wildlife record- ing, a wow and flutter content of 0.2 per cent would be quite acceptable, but an atmosphere recording incorporat- ing distant church bells should be approached with caution. Whilst the wildlife sound would be perfectly satisfactory, the wow on the church bells could ruin the whole effect.

Most reel-to-reel machines are equipped with a number of different playing speeds and an examination of the specification will show that invariably the percentage wow and flutter is progressively lower the higher the tape speed used. There are many other reasons why the highest tape speed possible should be used for wildlife sound recording but this one alone calls for the invariable use of the highest tape speed of which the machine is capable.

The second function of the transport system is to carry the spools of tape, releasing tape from the left-hand spool at a smooth rate and respooling it on the right-hand reel after it has passed the heads. These functions must be carried out without snatching or spilling, and without im- peding the true constant speed of the tape past the heads. It will be evident that the speed of the spools must vary depending on the amount of tape wound on to each side, and these differences in speed are accomplished by using various forms of clutch drive.

A system of brakes must also be incorporated so that the spools do not unwind themselves when the machine is not in use. The brakes are also important when the deck is switched into fast forward or reverse wind. During this process the spools revolve much faster than during playing or recording conditions and have much greater inertia. When the driving force is removed, the spool carrying the most tape would tend to free-wheel longer, and without brakes the tape would either spill when wound in one direction or stretch or even snap when wound in the other direction.

The tape is driven across the heads by being held firmly against a rotating cylinder or capstan by a rubber wheel termed the pinch roller. Releasing the pressure on the pinch roller will immediately allow the capstan to slip on the tape so that the tape can be made to stop, even though the capstan continues to rotate and is ready to draw the tape on again the moment the pinch roller pressure is restored. This is often deliberately used as a pause feature and is very useful to the wildlife sound recordist, as machine run-up time is practically eliminated and yet tape is not wasted. The pinch wheel is also withdrawn, of course, during fast wind operations and when the machine is at rest. This latter feature is most important because if the pinch wheel is left in stationary contact with the capstan it can develop a flat spot which will later cause wow and flutter when the machine is used again.

All these functions can be driven by one motor using a system of belt drives which are adjusted mechanically to suit each mode of operation. Usually the adjustment is done through a series of levers directly under control of the operator, but sometimes solenoid operation is incorporated, energized by the operator by means of key-operated micro switches.

Many mains machines employ a number of motors, usually three, and these simplify or eliminate the mechanical selection problems. However, most modern portables use one motor to save weight.

To keep the tape in intimate contact with the heads during record and playback, small pressure pads are often fitted and are coupled to the lever operating the pinch roller so that they are automatically withdrawn during fast wind operations.

If the layout of tape guides and heads is such that the tape automatically tends to be pulled against the heads, then pressure pads may not be required. In such designs the tape would always be in contact with the heads even during fast wind operations, and some designers, arguing that this will cause unnecessary wear, incorporate a means whereby the tape is held away from the heads during these operations. One designer argues that during fast wind operations a layer of air builds up between the head and tape in a similar manner to car wheels on a wet surface which aquaplane at high speed. His decks do not show evidence of rapid head wear, so he could be right.

The heart of the deck is the motor driving the capstan which, in the absence of other motors, must also simultaneously drive the take-up spool and during fast wind operations must be mechanically coupled to either spool. But its quality depends on its use as a drive for the capstan, as it is evident that cyclic variations of speed are the source of wow and flutter.

It was general practice at one time, and is still common, to find that a heavy flywheel is incorporated to help smooth out these cyclic variations of speed. The weight of the flywheel can be reduced if its speed of rotation is increased, and as the flywheel usually rotates at the same speed as the capstan, this explains why the wow and flutter are usually at their lowest when the machine operates at its fastest speed. In a portable, apart from the disadvantage of carrying a heavy flywheel, movement of the machine can affect the flywheel itself and some machines are more prone to this defect than others.

General speed control of a mains machine is usually achieved by using a synchronous motor which, like the speed of an electric clock, is governed by the frequency of the mains supply. As this never varies much more than a few per cent, to all intents and purposes the machine speed may be regarded as being constant.

The case of a portable is very different as we are dependent on batteries whose terminal voltage can vary considerably. The motor speed would vary accordingly if it were coupled directly to the battery. Many means have been adopted in the past to achieve constant speed during the life of the battery, and the means adopted has a bearing on the price of the machine. The cheapest method is to rely on a fairly simple transistorized circuit which ensures that, within limits, no matter what the state of the batteries, a constant voltage supply is sustained at the motor terminals. At the other extreme, a small tacho generator is attached to the motor and its output will therefore depend on the speed. This same output is fed back to a transistorized control board feeding the motor and hence controls the supply to the motor. This is a servo system and very fine speed control can be achieved, but the control board is complicated and expensive. The same system is sometimes used on mains machines, the capstan motor being DC driven to achieve a true speed independent of mains frequency.

The number of heads depends on the electronics used. The heads are arranged so that the first one met by the tape is the erase head, which is present to clean off any recordings already on the tape when it is desired to make a new recording. This is a demagnetizing process and a fairly wide gap is employed in order to produce a strong magnetic field. The field is created by passing an alternating current through the winding. This alternating field must be of high frequency because each segment of tape

The Uher CR210 compact cassette, probably the best cassette machine for wildlife sound recording. Light and small, this machine can be used for recording in mono or stereo. (*Photo:* Uher)

The Uher 4200 Report IC. A lightweight, quality reel-to-reel portable shown in half track stereo form. Four speeds are selected by the gate at the right-hand side. The controls are well laid out; optional extras include an ever-ready case and a rechargeable battery. (*Photo:* Uher)

Hand holding a reflector; the author demonstrates home-made equipment. The 508 mm x 127 mm (20 in. x 5 in.) focal length reflector is moulded in fibreglass flexibly attached to a comfortable pistol grip carved in hard wood while the microphone is flexibly mounted inside the windshield. (*Photo:* 3M)

Using a mono-pod mount. The mono-pod consists of a broom handle used to support a Grampian 609 mm x 203 mm (24 in. x 8 in.) focal length reflector in spun aluminium. The microphone is a Grampian DP6 dynamic. (*Photo:* 3M)

must be subject to several cycles before it passes onwards and the actual movement of the tape causes the necessary decaying field to avoid any residual magnetism on the tape. Up to two watts of power are required by the erase head to effectively wipe the tape clean and the wave form must be as pure sinusoidal as possible. This power is developed by the oscillator section of the pre-amplifier.

Sometimes on cheaper machines the erase head is replaced by a permanent magnet which is mechanically brought into contact with the tape during erasure. This effectively removes the previously recorded signal but usually leaves some magnetism which results in a hiss when the tape is replayed. This system is satisfactory for dictating machines where the microphone is held close to the lips and in any case recording quality is unimportant, but if such a machine were to be used for wildlife sound recording where the signal is much weaker, the hiss would be too prominent to permit a good recording. However, provided clean tape is used, the magnet can be removed and satisfactory recordings can be made. One point in favour of such a machine is that the pre-amplifier is simplified and places a much reduced drain on the power supply.

The second and third heads are respectively the record and playback heads, but in many machines a common dual-purpose head is used instead of two separate heads. Separate heads mean that the recorded signal can be played back immediately after the signal has been recorded. Thus the recordist can check immediately on the quality of the recording whereas with the dual-purpose head, his only check on quality during recording is by referring to the instrument's meter.

The magnetic gap width of the head is all-important. The gap of a playback head must be kept as narrow as possible to ensure good high-frequency response, but for recording purposes there is a limit to the narrowness of the gap; if it is too narrow, a recording magnetic field strong enough to saturate the tape cannot be produced. Thus if a common record/playback head is used, the gap is something of a compromise and the overall record/playback frequency response cannot be expected to be quite as good as when separate heads are used. Thus the use of separate heads for record and playback is to be preferred although, inevitably, separate heads mean more costly machines, the price being determined not only by the additional head but by the construction of the amplifier.

A little thought will show that the gaps on the record and playback heads must be parallel to each other so that the signal is picked up exactly in the same way as it was recorded. To allow the tape to be played back on any other machine, the gap must be at right angles to the tape. Accordingly these heads (or the common head) are mounted so that they may be rocked by an adjusting screw. This is referred to as adjusting the azimuth. If tapes recorded on one machine do not play back successfully on another machine, and both machines are known to be in full working order, it is certain that the azimuth on at least one of the machines is out of adjustment.

The depth of the gap may be practically equal to the full width of the tape, nearly half the width, or even less than a quarter of the width, giving rise to the terms full track, half track or quarter track. The wider the track used the better will be the signal-to-noise ratio, so full track is generally used whenever possible on all professional machines.

The half-track machine was originally devised to make some economy in the use of tape, especially for the domestic user who would accept a slightly worse signal-to-noise ratio. The half-track heads are arranged to record and play back the top half of the tape as it moves across the head from left to right. The spool is then turned over and a second recording is made on the lower half of the tape, which of course is now at the top. A slight space called a guard is necessary between the two tracks to avoid the two recorded signals being replayed together, so that the half-track recording is, in fact, slightly narrower than half full-track. With the introduction of stereo recording, both tracks are recorded simultaneously as the tape passes from left to right, the upper track being used for the left-hand channel and the lower track for the right-hand channel. At first two half-track heads were used, but maintaining their exact distance apart, essential to ensure correct phasing, was a problem; it was rapidly overcome by combining both gaps into the same head in exact vertical alignment.

Mono half-track recorded tapes can be replayed on a stereo half-track machine provided the right-hand channel is made dead. Without this precaution the lower gap will pick up the signal from the bottom track and replay it 'in reverse' on the right-hand channel. Ideally both channels should be coupled to the top track so that both loudspeakers receive an identical signal and the sound appears to emanate from a point midway between them. Many stereo recorders already incorporate switching to give this facility but the system is not immediately mono/stereo compatible.

As tape and heads continued to improve, the quarter-track machine was introduced to make even further economies of tape. In order to record and play back all four tracks in mono fashion, not only was the tape turned over but the height of the head was also adjusted so that in one position it picked up the two outer tracks and in another the two inner tracks. Machines of this type are now comparatively rare or even extinct, but for stereo recording a second gap was introduced and the machine thus gives the same running time for quarter-track stereo as is given by the same tape recorded half-track mono and, presumably, on this ground, the quarter-track stereo machine has prospered. So that the quarter-track stereo machine can play back half-track stereo tapes, the two gaps are separated. Half-track mono recordings can be replayed on such a machine but, once again, care must be taken to avoid replaying the bottom track 'in reverse' at the same time.

The latest development in quarter-track recording consists of the four-track machine which, as its name implies, is capable of recording or playing back all four tracks simultaneously. The heads on these machines incorporate four separate gaps and the machine is aimed at the quadraphonic enthusiast.

To differentiate between these different track configurations it has become customary to write mono full-track as 1/1, mono half-track as 1/2, mono quarter-track as 1/4, stereo half-track as 2/2, stereo quarter-track as 2/4 and quadrasonic quarter-track 4/4.

All these track configurations apply to reel-to-reel machines using standard-width tape which is 6.25 mm wide. Tapes of greater widths and many more tracks are used in recording studios, but these are beyond the scope of this book.

The compact cassette employs tape 3.81 mm wide. Half-track stereo recording was rejected at the outset and all machines are either half-track mono or quarter-track stereo. Compared with reel-to-reel there is one important difference in the position of tracks used to make a stereo pair. On cassettes the two head gaps are arranged one above the other, separated only by a guard gap. In consequence, when a half-track mono recording is replayed on a stereo machine, only one track can be picked up by both the gaps and the sound immediately emanates from the point midway between the speakers without any adjustment or switching being required. The system is, therefore, truly mono/stereo compatible.

The wildlife sound recordist who chooses the cassette

format thus has little choice in track configuration. If all considerations dictate that he must use this format, then he must accept the penalties of inherently poor signal-to-noise ratio. There are certain improvements still available such as using low-noise tape and, perhaps, noise-reduction systems, but, as will be seen later, not all these systems are entirely suitable for this kind of recording.

The reel-to-reel user has a choice. The usual process of editing (see Chapter 11) dictates that tape should be run past the heads once only so that, ideally, full-track should be used for mono (1/1) and half-track (2/2) for stereo recording, thereby conferring the best signal-to-noise ratio in each case. As full-track is only available on professional machines, the ideal for mono recording is bound to be expensive and most wildlife sound recordists settle for half-track. As a half-track stereo machine (2/2) can be used for recording half-track mono with practically the same results or even 'double mono', this is probably the best choice as it leaves the options open for recording mono or stereo even if initially the recordist only wishes to record in mono.

The quarter-track machine cannot be recommended because of its inferior signal-to-noise ratio, and in view of the comments already made on editing, would confer no economy in the use of tape. Apart from these considerations, 'drop-outs' are much more likely to be experienced. A drop-out is caused by a slight twist occurring in the tape as it travels from the spool to the record head which can result in a momentary loss of contact between the tape and the head. The narrower the track width the more likely is it that the drop-out will be noticeable.

AMPLIFIER

The complete amplifier comprises a number of definable stages through which the signal is processed. The record chain of events for a mono recorder is illustrated in block form in Fig. 5(a). In Fig. 5(b) the playback chain is illustrated. Stereo machines require each part of the chain to be duplicated, although the oscillator is common.

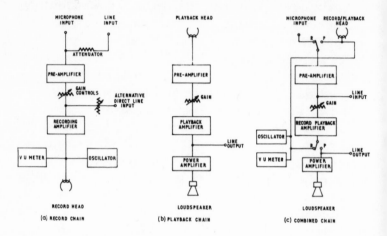

Fig. 5 Recorder amplifiers

If the recorder is fitted with separate record and playback heads, both these chains must exist as completely separate entities so that the record and playback processes may proceed at the same time.

If a common record/playback head is used, only one chain can be used at a time, and as the majority of components in the microphone pre-amplifier and recording amplifier are similar to those used in the headlift and playback pre-amps, simple switching can convert the amplifiers and result in a considerable economy. The combined chain is thus shown in Fig. 5(c).

PREAMPLIFIER The strength of the microphone signal will vary enormously depending on the sensitivity of the microphone in use and the sound pressures to which it is subjected, but compared with high-level signals derived from a radio tuner, gramophone or another tape recorder, the strength is extremely weak.

The purpose of the pre-amplifier is, therefore, to faithfully increase the microphone signal comparable to that of other high-level signals and thus provide a signal of adequate strength for driving ensuing stages. To perform its function correctly it must be capable of amplifying a wide range of signal strengths covering the full audio frequency spectrum, and to do this without distortion and without adding any significant amount of noise.

Noise has already been mentioned in Chapter 3, referring to capacitor microphones which incorporate their own pre-amplifier without which the microphone signal would be too weak to feed the recorder pre-amplifier. The problems of noise afflict the recorder pre-amplifier with even greater force when it is realized that it should cater for any type of microphone and thus a wide range of sensitivities. Designing such a pre-amplifier is not easy, and except in the very best recorders, compromises are made in the interest of economy. For example, some restriction may be placed on the models of microphone that may be used and it may be assumed that only general sounds such as speech and music will be recorded. These subjects will generally produce a good signal-to-noise ratio, but with much weaker signals it may be unacceptable. On the other hand, if designed to produce a good signal-to-noise ratio with a weak signal, severe distortion may result if a strong signal is applied.

In general the sounds recorded from wildlife are weak and often interspersed with periods of silence. It is during these periods of relative quiet that the noise makes itself most obvious, although even then it may be masked by a high ambience. Thus, in certain conditions, the recordist may resort to the use of an external microphone pre-amplifier, the design and use of which is discussed in Chapter 6.

It will be noted that the pre-amplifer has a fixed gain, and sooner or later some device must be introduced whereby the strength of the signal ultimately fed to the record head can be controlled. This is generally achieved by adjusting the strength of the signal at the output of the pre-amplifier before it is passed on to the record amplifier. This device thus controls the effective gain of the pre-amplifier and is termed the gain control. If the gain control was placed before the pre-amplifier its noise would be amplified, and if it was operated during record-ing would produce a dreadful crackle.

In Fig. 5(a) it will be noted that high-level signals are reduced in strength or attenuated before being passed to the pre-amplifier, otherwise they could cause severe over-load distortion. Alternatively, in better-class machines, these high-level inputs are fed into the record amplifier via a separate gain control, thus making it possible to record signals from such a source and the microphone simultaneously. The relative settings of the two gain con-trols effectively mix the signals in any desired ratio. This is a useful facility, particularly on a mains machine, when it is to be used for copying and it is wished to add a com-mentary, but it has little value on a field recorder. How-ever, as will be seen in Chapter 6, this method of connection enables external microphone pre-amplifiers to be used to the best effect.

RECORDING AMPLIFIER Signals from the microphone pre-amplifier and other inputs are fed to the recording amplifier for further amplification, during which process frequency compensation is introduced to allow for the non-linear magnetic induction process. This non-linearity results from a combination of a number of factors and, even with the same head and tape, varies with tape speed. If no compensation were introduced, the final output would sound like that produced by a telephone and the designer must introduce components into the record and playback amplifiers to boost the treble and often the bass frequencies as well, so that there is no perceptible difference between the original and recorded sound. If this is done correctly the machine can be stated to have an overall level response.

The compensation process is referred to as equalizing and the components used are called an equalizing network. It would be extremely convenient if it were possible to carry out the complete process during recording so that the playback amplifier would only need a level response, but unfortunately the amount of boost is limited by other considerations and in practice some equalization must still be performed during playback.

If a tape recorded on one machine is to be played back on another, the amount of boost given during record and playback should be the same on both machines. The playback machine's tone controls can be manipulated to take into account any differences, but this presupposes that the listener is well aware of how the recording should sound. To facilitate the exchange of tapes, standards for the degree of boost applied during each process have been formulated and fix the amount of boost to be applied during playback as this is easy to define and check. Once the playback equalization is fixed, the designer must adjust the record equalization so that overall level response is achieved. The playback equalizing network can be shown to have a time constant, so the standards simply lay down the time constants to be used at each speed.

Over the years the recommended time constants have changed as tape and heads have improved, and at the same time there have been attempts to rationalize the recommendations between one country and another so that nowadays most European national and international standards (CCIR, BSI and DIN) are in agreement for most speeds. However, in America (NARTB, sometimes abbreviated to NAB) the time constants are different. In spite of their own national standards, many European manufacturers prefer to use the NAB standard or at least offer it as an alternative, and even when the recording standard is chosen, very often facilities are provided for playing back tapes to either standard. The important thing to remember is that the lower the time constant employed the greater will be the recorded treble boost, and if such tapes are played back with a higher time constant, the treble will be over-emphasized and the recording will sound too brilliant.

Another function of the record amplifier is to drive the recorder's level indicator which nowadays takes the form of a meter. There are two types of meter in general use, the VU or volume unit meter and the PPM or peak programme meter. The VU meter is most commonly employed because the meter and its electronics, consisting of a simple rectifier circuit, are both cheap compared with the PPM. The performance of each type of meter is laid down in international standards which decree that the VU meter shall take 300 milliseconds for its needle to reach 99 per cent of its full deflection for that particular strength of signal, whereas the PPM takes only 12 milliseconds to register full deflection. The PPM is thus a much faster operating device and its return to zero when the signal is removed must be slowed down or the needle action would be a blurr. Such an instrument requires careful design with very low inertia, efficient damping, etc. In addition, the PPM scaling is logarithmic, making it far easier to read in the crucial areas of full modulation. By contrast the VU meter has a simple scale and the needle rises and falls at about the same speed, which gives the impression that it is operating faster than a PPM.

The songs of many species of birds such as the robin and the wren contain peaks of sound of shorter duration than 300 milliseconds and these peaks will therefore register only partially on a VU meter. If the gain of the recorder is set so that the longer phrases of the song give a high reading on the meter, it is almost certain that the peaks will over-modulate the tape. Very often the peaks can fully modulate the tape even though the VU meter has scarcely shown any reading throughout the recording.

Thus the readings of a VU meter need careful interpretation and under these circumstances a PPM would be a considerable improvement. However, the luxury of using one in the field is largely denied us by the manufacturers.

OSCILLATOR The output from the recording amplifier is fed to the record head where it is mixed with the HF bias derived from the oscillator.

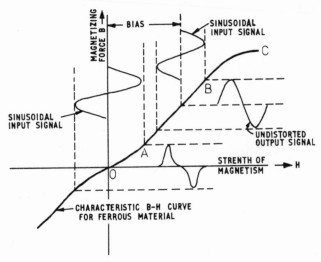

Fig. 6 Graphical illustration of DC bias (AC bias has similar effect)

Fig. 6 shows the need for bias. This is a typical magnetization curve and shows that over a considerable portion it is not linear. That is to say, doubling the magnetizing force does not double the amount of magnetization. Between *A* and *B* there is a direct relationship and it is between these points that we must operate to avoid distortion. From *B* to *C* the result will be over-recording or over-modulation. Between *O* and *A* there would also be distortion, but the HF bias raises the magnetization to *A* before the signal is superimposed. The shape of the curve is typical but varies from one make of tape to another and the exact amount of bias has to be adjusted for each make to ensure distortionless recording.

Reference has already been made to the oscillator when discussing the erase head. Obviously the oscillator must produce a frequency way above the frequency of any audio signal. In early times a frequency of 20 kHz was considered sufficient, but nowadays frequencies of 80 kHz and even higher are often employed. To effectively erase old recordings, up to 2 watts of power are required and the wave form must be pure. Only about 60 milliwatts of power are required for the bias power so that there is something to be said for eliminating the erase head on a portable altogether and limiting the oscillator power to that required for the bias. However, we have not yet encountered a commercially produced portable that does not have erase facilities even if they are only of the permanent magnet variety.

The recording chain is now complete and we must examine the playback facilities.

HEAD-LIFT PRE-AMP Like the microphone pre-amplifier, this pre-amplifier is designed to give very high gain to minute signals, this time the signals being those generated in the playback head as the magnetized tape is drawn across the gap. Once again noise introduced at this stage is a major consideration in the design. The result is almost identical to that of the microphone amplifier, and if the recorder is not required to record and play back at the same time, a single pre-amplifier can be suitably switched to serve in either role.

PLAYBACK AMPLIFIER The playback amplifier is very similar to the record amplifier; apart from a variation in a relatively small number of components concerned with equalization, there is no difference. Therefore, once again if the recorder is not required to record and play back at the same time, the same amplifier can be used for both functions, the necessary change in the small number of components required being achieved as the amplifier is switched.

The playback amplifier feeds a line-out socket in parallel with the power amplifier. The line-out socket may be coupled to an external amplifier of greater power than the recorder's own amplifier in order to drive a better speaker system, or it may be connected to the line-input socket of another recorder which is being used to copy the tape being played on the first recorder.

POWER AMPLIFIER Many mains machines do not have a power amplifier, in which case the machine is termed a tape deck. It is reasoned that the user will already possess a high-quality amplifier and the tape deck is therefore an addition to an existing hi-fi installation. Portables usually incorporate a fairly low-power amplifier of 500 mW to 2 W capacity and a small speaker which is useful for quickly checking a recording in the field and can also be used for the call-down technique described in Chapter 7.

NOISE REDUCTION SYSTEMS, ETC.

To the fundamental electronics of a recorder it has become fashionable to look for certain added facilities such as limiters, automatic gain and noise reduction systems and we must briefly examine these facilities.

AUTOMATIC GAIN CONTROL (AGC)

Nowadays in addition to manual gain control many recorders incorporate automatic gain control (AGC). In the interests of economy many cheap cassette recorders dispense with the manual control and rely entirely on AGC. When AGC is switched in, over-modulation should be impossible, and therefore the system should be ideal for live recording. However, other features of the system make it unsuitable for most forms of wildlife recording.

As each sound peak occurs, AGC instantly reduces the gain and prevents the peak from causing over-modulation. Once the peak has passed, AGC slowly increases the gain at a predetermined rate up to a maximum. If in the meantime another peak occurs which would result in over-modulation with the gain at its present level, AGC reduces the gain for a second time and afterwards once more starts to increase the gain at the same rate as before. The time taken to increase the gain is fixed by the components in the circuit, but sometimes these are switchable to give a number of time constants. It is evident that if there were no time delay, all sounds would be recorded at the same level.

In practice the system works very well provided the dynamic range is not too great, but as most forms of wildlife sound recording include relatively long periods of comparative silence, the dynamic range *is* too great. During these periods of relative quiet, AGC increases the gain, resulting in a 'creeping' ambience and the result is completely unacceptable.

DOLBY

Tape hiss or noise is normally constant in magnitude and is therefore most noticeable when weak signals are replayed. Loud signals swamp the noise which then passes without notice. In other words, the signal-to-noise ratio varies with the signal strength, being poorest for weak signals.

The Dolby noise reduction system is designed to keep a constant signal-to-noise ratio irrespective of signal strength and it achieves this object by first sensing the signal strength and then adjusting the recording gain accordingly. On playback the signals are automatically adjusted in volume to their correct respective values, the recorded noise likewise being adjusted by the same amount.

The first system developed, now known as Dolby A, covers the full audio spectrum and the equipment is so expensive that it must be very rarely used outside professional recording studios where, however, it is now used extensively. However, a second, simplified, version known as Dolby B was developed to operate for frequencies above 1 kHz and this system is so much cheaper that it is now being incorporated in many mains machines and even into portable cassette recorders. Owing to their low tape speed and narrow tracks, cassette recorders have not hitherto been renowned for good signal-to-noise ratios, but the Dolby B system has improved their performance so much that a new aura of respectability has descended on them. For reel-to-reel recorders running at 190 mm/s tape hiss was already at a very low level, but with Dolby B it is quite inaudible.

From the explanation of how Dolby operates it is clear that any recordings 'encoded' by Dolby must be 'decoded' on playback. 'Decoding' any recording that has not been 'encoded' only results in a form of distortion.

The merits of the Dolby B system for wildlife sound recording are debatable and its success or otherwise depends to some extent on the type of subject being recorded. Many wildlife subjects consist of sounds interspersed with intervals of almost total silence and the application of Dolby B to such a recording is noticeable.

This indicates that the use of Dolby on subjects having a very wide dynamic range should be avoided. There are, however, many wildlife subjects to which it could probably be applied effectively.

Another noise reduction system operating in a similar manner to Dolby and called the ANRS (Automatic Noise Reduction System) has been developed more recently in Japan. It is claimed to be compatible with Dolby so that tapes encoded to this system can be played back with Dolby or vice versa. Under the circumstances there is no reason to believe that ANRS would be any more successful than Dolby B for wildlife sound recording.

DYNAMIC NOISE LIMITER (DNL)

This is another form of noise reduction system, this time developed by Philips with cassette recording in mind, but it can equally be applied to reel-to-reel recorders.

The system is designed to operate only on playback, which is a further advantage over Dolby and makes the equipment cheaper. The combined signal containing hiss is first fed to a phase splitter producing two identical signals, each of opposite phase. One of these signals is then further processed so that the wanted high-amplitude signals are severely attenuated but the low-amplitude signals associated with hiss and noise are unaffected. This processed signal is then re-combined with the other half of the original signal, but because the two are in opposite phase, the noise and hiss cancel each other out and the wanted signal is largely unaffected.

A similar degree of noise reduction is claimed as for Dolby B, but unlike Dolby the process is continuous, being unaffected by the strength of the wanted signal. It is therefore suitable for all forms of recording.

A number of recorders are available incorporating this system, but as it is unnecessary to have the equipment for record purposes, it is not usually found in a portable. It can, however, be used as a separate unit between a portable and an external amplifier.

LIMITERS

The limiter merely prevents peak signals from causing over-modulation. It will not operate at all unless the gain control is set high enough to produce peaks above normal recording level. On the other hand, if the gain control is set even higher it can be in operation for most of the time and all signals so treated will be recorded at the same level. Its use, therefore, is not recommended.

RECORDER SELECTION

The foregoing brief description of how a tape recorder operates is intended to make specifications more readily understood and the ultimate choice of machine less a matter of chance. Recorders represent the biggest single capital outlay, so their choice is a matter for serious consideration.

THE FIELD RECORDER

The choice of recorder for field work may well depend on whether the recordist already possesses a mains recorder. It is, however, not good policy to choose one field recorder in preference to another because it is apparently better at playing back tapes. It may have a larger loudspeaker and more powerful amplifier output to drive it, even a tone control, but it will probably not function any better as a recorder and the playback cannot equal that from a good mains machine. The larger case needed and extra weight of speaker, etc. all have to be carried in the field unnecessarily.

In the absence of a mains machine even the most modest portable can produce a better playback sound if an external speaker is used and, even better, if a line output is fed to an external mains amplifier and loudspeaker.

Sooner or later, however, the recordist should invest in a mains machine. It will not only play back tapes much better than a portable but will be found much more suitable for editing tapes, and makes copying possible.

OPEN-REEL OR CASSETTE?

Until recently only reel-to-reel recording was considered satisfactory when quality was of prime importance, but there are now a number of cassette portables claiming professional specifications which a few years ago would have been respectable for even reel-to-reel machines. Most of these machines cost nearly as much as, or even more than, good reel-to-reel machines and are just as heavy and bulky; they usually incorporate noise-reduction systems to compensate for the inherently inferior signal-to-noise performance of cassettes compared with open-reel. As noted earlier, noise-reduction systems are not recommended for wildlife sound recording, so the same money spent on a reel-to-reel machine would be a better investment.

Another point in favour of reel-to-reel recording is that the original tape can be edited with ease whereas a cassette must first be copied on to standard tape and ultimately any copy made for presentation will be another generation removed from the original with a further, if very slight, deterioration of the signal.

A few years ago there were many more reel-to-reel portables available but the choice is now severely limited. The three makes most readily available are the Uher, Tandberg and Nagra.

Nagra offer a number of machines built to the very highest of professional standards which are generally regarded as being too expensive for the amateur. Their normal machines are available in mono or stereo and are heavy compared with the other two makes, but an unusual model, the SN, is both light and almost minute, owing these features to the use of tape similar to that used in cassettes but operating on the reel-to-reel principle. If its price were lower this model might well be an ideal one for the wildlife sound recordist. Their normal machines usually have a tape speed of 380 mm/s thus meeting the most exacting scientific requirements. The SN operates at a fixed speed of 95 mm/s.

The Tandberg Series 11 is a first-class mono recorder offering full professional facilities such as off-track monitoring. The machine is lighter than the conventional Nagra machine but comparable in size. The top tape speed is 190 mm/s.

The Uher reel-to-reel machines are available in mono or stereo form, the latter in either double or four-track. If stereo is required the double-track model is the obvious choice for wildlife recording, giving the better signal-to-noise ratio. The Uher is the lightest portable reel-to-reel machine among those listed, and is capable of exceptionally good results. Rechargeable batteries are available and although costly, they can represent a saving on the purchase of batteries if the machine is to be used a great deal. Top speed is 190 mm/s.

If all these are too expensive, secondhand versions can sometimes be found and there are also a number of excellent obsolete models such as the EMI L4 and Grundig TK3300. Spares for obsolete models may be something of a problem.

Among the most expensive cassette machines are the Nakamichi 550, the JVC 1635, the Sony TC153SD and the Uher CR120, all of which are stereo and have excellent specifications, but only the Uher CR210 can claim to show any significant saving in weight and size over the smallest quality reel-to-reel machine. All except the Uher CR210 incorporate noise-reduction systems, the use of which is debatable for wildlife sound recording. Thus if quality is desired albeit with a somewhat inferior signal-to-noise ratio, coupled with minimum weight, the Uher CR210 must be the obvious choice.

For the beginner with limited means, there are many more cassette models to chose from, all at a fraction of the price of a good reel-to-reel machine. Of course, these cannot compare with the performance of the reel-to-reel type or even to the expensive cassette machines referred to above. It is, however, rather disappointing that the vast majority of cassette recorders at the cheaper end of the market are fully automatic and it is becoming almost impossible to find a cheap cassette recorder with manual control. This is a pity because slightly more expensive machines offering a choice of manual or automatic control are usually larger and heavier.

There are so many cassette machines available that no specific recommendations can be made, particularly as new machines are constantly appearing and older models being withdrawn. In making a choice the following considerations should be taken into account:

Weight. Cassette machines can vary from about two to six kilograms. Good reel-to-reel recorders weigh approximately six to ten kilograms and are found by many to be too heavy. It is important for the machine to be fitted with batteries when its weight is being assessed.

Batteries. Make sure the types specified are generally available and offer a reasonable running time for the minimum cost.

Carrying case. The case should offer reasonable protection to the machine and yet make it possible to gain access to the tape and controls. The strap should be adequately strong and be padded to spread the weight on the shoulder.

Controls. Ideally these should be convenient for operation when the machine is slung on the shoulder and in this position the recordist should have a clear view of the

VU meter. The VU meter on many cassette machines is often situated in a position more suitable for when the machine is laid flat.

Monitoring facilities. Sometimes it is not possible to adjust the record level except during actual recording and this is something of a disadvantage.

Tape type changeover facilities. Portables are now available capable of using chromium dioxide tape and this may be considered an advantage, although modern 'sandwich' cassette tapes give almost equally good results without the need to change the bias.

Many machines offer additional facilities such as built-in microphones etc., none of which are necessary for wildlife sound recording and only add unnecessary complications and extra weight.

THE MAINS MACHINE

The need for a reel-to-reel mains machine has been stressed frequently in this chapter and here the choice is much wider. There has, however, been a marked decrease in recent years in favour of mains cassette machines which are not suitable for the purpose of editing.

It is, of course, essential that the mains machine should have a top speed at least equal to that of the field recorder if the latter is a reel-to-reel model. There is something to be said for having a top speed even higher, because although the frequency recorded in the field cannot be improved, when it comes to copying it is often found better to copy at an even higher speed.

The tracking arrangements should be at least as good as in the field recorder.

Perhaps one of the most important aspects of the mains machine should be its performance as an editing deck. Inching facilities, interjection, variable speed rewind, are all very desirable features although usually found only on professional machines. Even without these features, however, there are still quite a large number of suitable machines available. It is difficult to make specific recommendations, but the names Ferrograph and Revox come readily to mind. Ferrograph has the advantage of being British and one can't help feeling that the company is near at hand for advice and service should this be necessary.

If the recordist already possesses a good amplifier he may not wish to buy a complete recorder as a deck would suffice and would be cheaper. On the whole, however, it is better to have a complete recorder that can be used on its own, as the saving in cost is not usually very great.

Sometimes good-quality transport systems can be obtained quite cheaply and the enthusiast who possesses a good amplifier can construct a simple pre-amplifier to enable the machine to be used for playback and editing. A suitable pre-amplifier circuit is shown in Fig. 7. This is simple to build and can be accommodated in a suitable-sized tobacco tin, thereby providing a good screen.

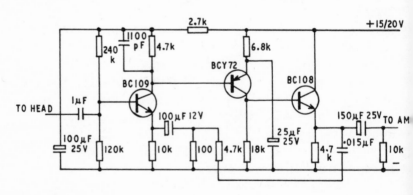

Fig. 7 Tape-head pre-amplifier equalized to CCIR playback at 190 mm/s.

TAPE

Before leaving this chapter a few words on the all-important matter of tape will be appropriate.

Each recorder manufacturer recommends in his instruction book the type of tape to be used with his machine to obtain the best results, and using the recommended tape is certainly safe. Changing to a different make or type of tape may well require adjustment to the bias, which is often a job for the expert and varies from one machine to another. Similar types but different makes may be tried, using the ear to judge whether the change is acceptable.

Most manufacturers of portable machines recommend long-play tape. On 130 mm reels this means that 270 metres of tape can be accommodated and at 190 mm/s this will run for about twenty-two minutes. This is an adequate playing time and the temptation to use thinner tape should be avoided because such tape is difficult to handle during editing.

The cassette user should concentrate on tapes offering the best frequency response coupled with low noise. Chromium dioxide tape is best for this purpose, but as it requires a much stronger bias, it is not suitable for all portables. However, the very latest generation of cassette tapes employ a combination of layers of ferric oxide and chromium dioxide and only require normal bias to give an improved frequency response and lower noise.

The popular sizes of cassette are, of course, the C.60, C.90 and C.120, each size related to the tape thickness. C.60 and C.90 sizes give ample recording time for the wildlife sound recordist and are generally reckoned to be more reliable than the C.120 size.

Further reading

British Standard 1568, *Magnetic Tape Recording Equipment*, BSI.

HELLYER, H. W., *Tape Recorders*, Fountain Press, 1970.

SPRING, P., *Tape Recorders: Performance, Analysis and Service Techniques*, Focal Press, 1967.

5

Reflectors

The subject of reflectors, their theory, construction and use or abuse, is surprisingly a subject discussed among wildlife sound recordists more often than any other single topic. Surprising, because the reflector is an inert piece of equipment, often quite crudely constructed, and one could be excused for thinking that there would be little to discuss. It is, however, one item of equipment that lends itself readily to the home constructor who must then decide for himself the shape and size, how to mount the microphone and how to use it. In this chapter we must examine all these problems.

Initially the device may be compared with a light reflector, a typical example being the car headlamp. This is a useful analogy because the effect of using a reflector with a lamp can actually be seen. Thus the car headlamp, by concentrating nearly all the light emitted from a relatively low powered lamp and projecting it forward into a single narrow beam, concentrates all the light power where it is needed and allows us to drive into the night at speeds which would clearly be impossible if it were not for the aid of the reflector. Alternatively, if some combustible material is fixed in the position of the lamp and the reflector pointed towards the sun, heat would be concentrated sufficiently to ignite the material.

It should be appreciated that the precise curve of the reflector must be such that all the light waves parallel to its axis are reflected from or to a common point known as the focal point. The surface that performs this function is parabolic in shape and therefore the curve conforms to the mathematical formula $y^2 = 4kx$; k is a constant and, in fact, the distance up the x axis from the origin to the focal point. Fig. 8 shows a number of parabolic curves, each one having different values of k. The greater the value of k the more shallow the curve becomes.

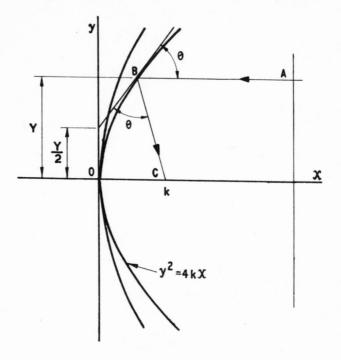

Fig. 8 Properties of the parabola

Light waves reflect from a polished surface, obeying the rule that the angle of reflection equals the angle of incidence. The fact that all the waves are returned to the focal point can be verified graphically by drawing tangents to the curve at points where a line parallel to the axis cuts the parabola. A tangent to a parabola is drawn easily and accurately if one realizes that the tangent will always cut the y axis at half the value of Y corresponding to the value of Y at the tangential point. By measuring the angle between the tangent and the horizontal line and then drawing a new line from the tangential point at the same angle, it will be noted that each new line passes through the same point corresponding to the k value.

While on the subject of graphics, it can be verified that length AB added to BC is always the same, showing that all light waves would have the same distance to travel and would therefore arrive simultaneously at the focal point.

As both light and sound waves normally travel in straight lines and sound can be reflected from a hard surface in just the same way as light is reflected from a bright or polished surface, one might be excused for thinking that all we have to do is to substitute a microphone for the lamp, making the reflector of the right material and big enough to concentrate sufficient sound, and that will be the end of the matter.

From a practical point of view, as we shall see, this is precisely what is done. However, before getting down to practical details we must first examine more closely the effects on a microphone caused by mounting it in a reflector.

Ideally the sound reflector/microphone combination should have a flat response curve over the required frequency range – corresponding, in fact, to the ideal of the perfect microphone described in Chapter 3. It is also highly desirable that its directional property should be maintained over the same frequency range. Unfortunately these ideals, achieved easily with a light reflector, are not achieved with a sound reflector, and no doubt this is because the wavelengths of sound are very long compared with those of light and are generally comparable in length to the diameter of the reflector.

To verify these facts Professor G. N. Patchett carried out a series of experiments. By setting up a variable-frequency sound source on the axis of a reflector he was able to measure the actual gain of the reflector. An identical open microphone was also used so that by subtracting the values recorded using the open microphone from those values recorded by the reflector combination, he had an exact measurement of the effects of the reflector.

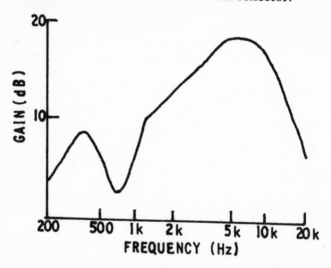

Fig. 9 Frequency response of omni-directional microphone in 609 mm (24 in.) diameter reflector of 178 mm (7 in.) focal length

Thus Fig. 9 shows the measured change in response of an omni-directional microphone when mounted in a 609 mm (24 in.)* reflector having a focal length of 178 mm (7 in.). Such a reflector has been on the market for some time, so the results should be of more than usual interest.

The first point to note is that at 200 Hz there is a gain of 5 dB. Many theorists have hitherto insisted that there can be no gain for frequencies whose wavelengths are more

* G. N. Patchett experimented with reflectors made to imperial dimensions.

than double the diameter of the reflector, yet at 200 Hz the wavelength is 1660 mm (5 ft 5½ in.)* Professor Patchett suggests that this gain may be due to diffraction rather than reflection.

At 600–700 Hz there is a dip of some 7 dB, thought to be due to the partial cancellation of the reflected wave by the direct sound waves. The reflected wave must travel 356 mm (14 in.) further than the direct wave, and this corresponds to half the wavelength at 466 Hz. Therefore, the maximum degree of cancellation should theoretically occur at this frequency.

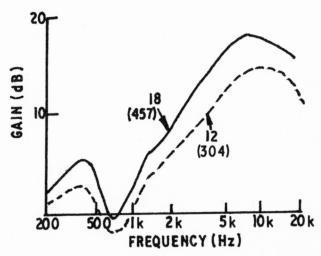

Fig. 10 Frequency response of omni-directional microphone in 457 mm (18 in.) and 304 mm (12 in.) diameter reflectors of 178 mm (7 in.) focal length

From 1 kHz to 10 kHz the gain increases in direct proportion to the frequency and this supports the theory that reflection only occurs when the wavelength is less than twice the diameter of the reflector. Thus as the frequency increases, more and more of the surface area of the reflector

*Wavelengths are based on speed of sound at 0°C, i.e. 332 metres per second.

comes into play and so the gain should go on increasing with frequency.

At 10 kHz the wavelength is 33 mm (1.3 in.) and this corresponds to the diameter of the microphone which is now effectively masking the reflector and preventing the gain from continuing. Professor Patchett proved the point by substituting a microphone of smaller diameter and the gain continued until the wavelength again corresponded with the smaller-diameter microphone.

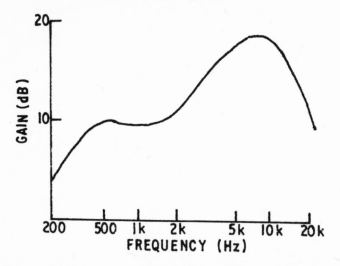

Fig. 11 Frequency response of omni-directional microphone in 609 mm (24 in.) diameter reflector of 101 mm (4 in.) focal length

Fig. 10 shows what happens when the same microphone is mounted in reflectors of 457 mm (18 in.) and 304 mm (12 in.) diameter but having the same focal length as before. As might be expected, these curves prove that the smaller the diameter the lower the gain, particularly at the lower frequencies. Perhaps the most remarkable feature is the response between 500 and 1000 Hz which, for a considerable range of frequencies, is actually less than is obtained using a completely open microphone. The smaller

the diameter of the reflector, the more extended this range
of frequencies becomes. The author believes the explanation is simply that the direct wave is stronger than the
reflected wave or, put another way, the reflected wave de-
tracts from the direct wave making the response worse than
an open microphone. Whatever the reasoning, the curves
show that reflectors of this diameter are useless for frequencies below 1000 Hz and in general use must lead to
the production of 'thin' or 'tinny' recordings. In general
it is not wise to use a reflector of less than 508 mm
(20 in.) diameter.

Fig. 11 shows what happens when the focal length is
reduced to 101 mm (4 in.). The dip due to the cancellation of reflected wave by direct wave is not so serious.
With a 101 mm (4 in.) focal length the theoretical cancellation frequency would be 900 Hz and by the time this
frequency is reached the gain resulting from reflection is
much greater than at 600–700 Hz. Hence the cancellation

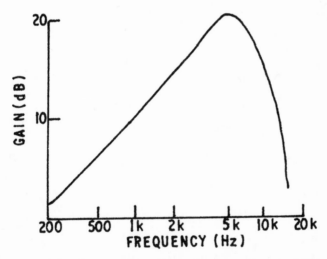

Fig. 12 Frequency response of cardioid microphone in 609 mm
(24 in.) diameter reflector of 178 mm (7 in.) focal length

effect is reduced. This would indicate that the focal length should be kept as low as possible.

Finally, Fig. 12 shows the change in response when a cardioid microphone is mounted in a reflector. As the cardioid microphone has very little response from sound waves approaching from the rear, there is no cancellation of the reflected wave by the direct wave.

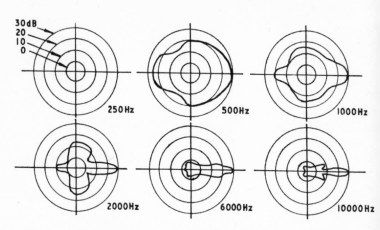

Fig. 13 Polar diagrams of a microphone in 609 mm (24 in.) diameter reflector of 178 mm (7 in.) focal length

To show the directional characteristics of a reflector Professor Patchett also measured the performance of the microphone/reflector combination when rotated relative to the sound source. The results are plotted on polar diagrams, a number of which are shown in Fig. 13. Each is plotted for the same frequency and the shapes show that the higher the frequency the more directional the instrument becomes.

The experiments show that provided the diameter and focal length are chosen with some care, the reflector gives a very worthwhile gain to the response of the same micro-

(*Above*) The author observing a colony of black-headed gulls on a moorland tarn. The gulls are well within recording distance.
(*Below*) Bempton Cliffs, Yorkshire – a good area for recording kittiwake, fulmar, guillemot, razorbill, puffin and gannet.

(*Above*) Leighton Moss, Lancashire – the reed beds here are the habitat of bittern, water rail, teal, wigeon, reed warbler and mammals such as water vole.

(*Below*) Surrey heathland – the habitat of nightingale, nightjar, stonechat, woodlark, skylark, meadow pipit, and a variety of mammals including deer, fox and badger.

phone used in open style and that it converts an omni-directional microphone into a highly sensitive directional instrument. The response, however, is not level, being relatively poor at low frequencies and again falling off at high frequencies. If it is intended to use an omni-directional microphone, the indications are that the reflector should have a relatively short focal length.

All the foregoing indicates that we should use as large a reflector as possible with a relatively short focal length. Reflectors up to 1200 mm in diameter, and even larger, have been used, but the difficulty of carrying and using such reflectors should be considered fully before embarking on such a size. Such reflectors generally need to be supported on a substantial tripod, thus adding yet a further item of equipment to be carried.

For the sole operator a reflector of more modest dimensions will be found more convenient. It will be easier to carry, much lighter, and can be held aloft with one hand. Taking all factors into account, a useful size is about 500 mm diameter with a focal length of one quarter the diameter. A focal length of one quarter the diameter places the microphone on the plane of the reflector so that a reasonable degree of shielding from the wind is provided without making the dish too deep. If the focal length is made shorter, while the response theoretically should be better and the wind protection further improved, the dish becomes deeper and inevitably heavier.

Commercially there is now a better choice open to the purchaser than ever before. In this country Grampian Reproducers Ltd were first in the field and their 609 mm (24 in.) by 178 mm (7 in.) focal length reflector in spun aluminium is still very popular. In the author's experience it is too large for easy carrying and the long focal length puts the microphone so far out that wind protection is an added problem. It has been argued that, being made of metal, it produces a tinny effect, but this may well be due

D

to the long focal length. Some users claim that this metallic ringing can be eliminated by covering the rear of the reflector with foam rubber. Professor Patchett demonstrated that the responses of a metal reflector and one made of fibreglass to the same dimensions were identical, so that the use of foam rubber on the rear of a metal reflector is probably a waste of time and certainly adds undesirable weight.

A range of fibreglass reflectors is now available from Sonic Instruments Ltd. These reflectors are very well made and incorporate a very good microphone suspension system.

The latest product is a 457 mm (18 in.) plastic reflector developed in Canada and marketed by Reslo Sound Ltd under the name of the Dan Gibson reflector. The reflector is supplied complete with an integral microphone and the whole is engineered to a very high standard. In one version there is a built-in amplifier, part of which serves to correct the inherent weaknesses in the reflector characteristic and results in a more level and extended response, while the other part gives an output sufficient to drive a pair of headphones. The assembly is exceptionally light in weight and the clear plastic allows the operator an almost unrestricted view of his subject. Understandably, the complete assembly is expensive and suffers a number of drawbacks, not the least of which is a tendency for the dish to warp, especially if left in a warm location.

Failing any of these sources of supply, the enthusiast must turn to making his own. This was necessary a few years ago if one was not satisfied with the Grampian. There is no doubt that making a reflector can be quite rewarding and money-saving.

The obvious choice of material is fibreglass and nowadays the materials are readily available from car accessory shops. Most of the work is in making the mould. Modelling clay, sand and cement have been used for this purpose.

The best way to produce the shape is to plot the desired curve, transfer it to a piece of 10 mm ply, cut it out, and adapt the 'back' portion to form what moulders call a strickle board. Rotating the board about its axis generates the solid shape. When the mould is complete the chopped strand matting and resin are applied to the surface in accordance with the fibreglass manufacturer's instructions. Before applying it to the mould it must be treated with a releasing agent; if this is not available, a thin coating of grease can be applied instead. Two layers should be sufficient with perhaps a little more to reinforce the crown and edge. Too much fibreglass will result in an unnecessarily heavy reflector; too little might result in premature failure. The skill in moulding is to strike the right balance between the two. The author's first fibreglass reflector weighed 1650 gm (3 lb 10 oz) and the latest weighs 760 gm (1 lb 11 oz).

These weights are, of course, inclusive of the handle and microphone mount, and, apart from keeping the weight of these accessories to a minimum, their design is quite important.

The author has usually found it more convenient to fashion the handle from a piece of wood curved to form a comfortable pistol grip. From this a mould could be made, with the final handle being made from fibreglass, but as this would scarcely produce any saving in weight, it is not considered worthwhile. The latest version is glued and screwed to a brass plate cut to form attachment 'ears' which are drilled to take grommets so that the bolts through the shell are rubber-insulated from the handle itself. This is calculated to assist in reducing handling noise.

The location of the handle is important. Ideally it should be placed so that the hand rests under the centre of gravity of the reflector when carrying a microphone. Too far away from this position and the recordist will forever be restraining the overturning moment. This is bound to result in fatigue and lead to handling noise in attempts to adjust the grip to a more comfortable position.

There are times when it is necessary to hold the reflector horizontally and the attachment of other handles has been considered. However, on these rare occasions it has been found sufficient to steady the reflector by gripping the edge with the other hand. It must be remembered, however, that once recording has started the hands must not be moved or handling noise will result.

The next consideration is the way in which the microphone should be mounted, and the author has experimented with different methods. The first mount consisted of a rod to which two spring clips were attached. These effectively kept the microphone in its correct position but the assembly was difficult to handle without causing handling noise. Some form of resilient mounting was obviously needed. By inserting rubber washers between the clips and the rod a big improvement was found, improved still further by more rubber washers on top of the clips so that the clip was virtually sandwiched between the two washers. This form of suspension is still in use. A further method consisted of two rods about 100 mm (4 in.) apart and spanned at intervals by stout rubber bands. The microphone is merely inserted between the rubber bands, suitably twisted in order to give the right tension. This form of suspension works very well indeed but it is difficult to ensure that the microphone is in its precise position and it was sometimes found to have wandered out of position during use.

Some means of directing the reflector on to the subject is necessary. A careful watch of the VU meter would indicate when the reflector is pointed correctly, but it is very difficult to watch the VU meter and the subject at the same time and many species must be recorded with the gain so low that the VU meter will hardly register. This phenomenon is dealt with in a later chapter, and here it is sufficient to note that reliance cannot be placed on the VU meter reading because it may be almost non-existent for a full depth recording. This, coupled with the difficulty of watching two things at once, must quickly rule out the method.

Headphones can give the ears a good indication, but judging by apparent volume is not always easy. The subject of monitoring with headphones is also dealt with in Chapter 7.

The most useful way to aim a reflector is to provide it with a peephole. The combination of headphones and peephole is probably the ideal, particularly if the headphones can be switched to off-tape monitoring once recording has actually started. There is then a visual and aural check on aiming and the quality of the recording is also monitored.

The peephole can simply consist of a hole about 12 mm diameter drilled through the reflector just above the microphone. A forward sight incorporated in the microphone mount should then make the aiming of the reflector perfect except for a minor degree of parallax which can be disregarded for all practical purposes.

The field of vision through such a small hole is somewhat limited, and even when the peephole is held close to the eye it is quite easy to lose the subject. A larger hole, it can be argued, reduces the area of the reflector and permits direct sound waves from the rear to impinge on the microphone more readily. Even a small hole can be the source of noise caused by a slight breeze blowing over the aperture. These possible arguments can be eliminated by inserting a 25 mm diameter disc of perspex into the reflector. The perspex disc can have a centre marker or even crossed lines similar to telescopic sights on a rifle, and be cemented in place. A small drawback to a perspex 'window' is that sometimes a mist forms on the window but this occasional defect is more than outweighed by its advantages.

The final lining up of the reflector/microphone assembly is worth a little effort so that the user will be confident that the microphone is in its optimum position and the forward sight correctly positioned.

Although we may know the theoretical focal point, the exact working surface of the microphone may not be so easy to determine. It is therefore necessary to experiment with its position. A suitable sound source is required, ideally an audio signal generator set at about 6 kHz. The reflector should then be mounted on a tripod, about ten metres away, the microphone fixed in its support and connected to the recorder. All this should be set up in the open on a windless day, carefully avoiding any walls or trees from which sound could be reflected.

The signal generator and the recorder should be switched on, and the reflector panned horizontally and vertically until the maximum VU reading is obtained. Then the microphone is moved backwards or forwards until once more the maximum VU reading is obtained. The microphone support should now be marked in some way so that the microphone can always be placed in the same position and the forward sight of the reflector adjusted so that it is lined up on the signal generator loudspeaker when viewed through the peephole.

The reflector offers a very good form of wind protection to the microphone. The microphone can, of course, be fitted with its own proprietary brand of windshield before mounting it in the reflector. If it is intended to use such a windshield, the mount in the reflector must be designed accordingly and the peephole or 'window' positioned further away from the centre line of the microphone to allow for the increased diameter of the microphone when fitted with its windshield.

Perhaps the best and cheapest form of windshield for

use with a reflector consists of a couple of layers of nylon netting covering the whole assembly. The two layers of netting should form a circle of a diameter somewhat larger than the diameter of the reflector. A length of elastic is sewn into the edge of the netting so that the whole can be stretched over the reflector, the microphone support holding the netting away from the reflector like a tent pole. Ideally the elastic should be taut enough to prevent the netting moving and causing handling noise and yet to allow the nylon to form radial folds.

Most proprietary forms of microphone windshield are moulded in reticulated foam in the form of a helmet that simply slides over the end of the microphone. Reticulated foam sheeting can also be obtained and a windshield constructed in this material instead of nylon netting, but of course this form of windshield completely obscures the peephole or 'window', and in the author's opinion the loss of this facility is too high a price to pay.

Further reading

PATCHETT, G. N., 'Microphone Reflectors', *Wireless World*, June 1973, and *Journal of Wildlife Sound Recording Society*, Vol. 1, No. 6.

6

Other Field Equipment

MICROPHONE PRE-AMPLIFIERS

A microphone pre-amplifier is an electronic device connected between the microphone and the tape recorder,
designed to boost and sometimes filter or control the frequency response of the microphone output.

In order to compensate for weak signals the temptation
is to use greater amplification than that normally afforded
by the use of the recorder's own pre-amp.

Unfortunately not only the wanted signal but also the
ambience is amplified, and the result all too often produces
an unreal background sound and the method is soon
abandoned. For recording insects in temporary captivity
where the ambience can be controlled, the use of the extra
gain of a microphone pre-amplifier can be justified. Care
must be taken, however, that when such recordings are
replayed, an unnatural monster is not created. Perhaps in
such circumstances the recordings are of more scientific
than general interest, for a sound scarcely audible to the
human ear is hardly likely to produce any evocative feel-
ings if played back many times larger than life. For scientific use such recordings may well reveal some hitherto
unknown behaviour pattern and are thus extremely useful
to the entomologist.

Chapter 4 described the function of the recorder's pre-
amplifier and reference was made to the use of an external
microphone pre-amplifier as a means of improving the
signal-to-noise ratio, particularly if the recorder's pre-

amplifier tends to be more noisy than average. However, it is not generally appreciated that such an improvement depends not only on the noise quality of the pre-amplifier but also on how it is connected. The only way to make any improvement is to ensure that the record amplifier is fed with a signal having an improved signal-to-noise ratio. Assuming that everything has been done to produce a strong signal – close approach, using a reflector, etc. – and yet the signal-to-noise ratio is still unacceptable, the next recourse must be to consider using a microphone pre-amplifier.

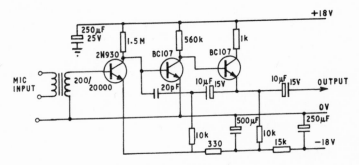

Fig. 14 Low-noise high-gain microphone pre-amplifier

If a microphone pre-amplifier having a similar gain to the recorder's pre-amplifier, but having less noise, is fed direct into the line input – see Fig. 5(a) – the problem is immediately solved. The microphone pre-amplifier can be designed to give even higher gain than the recorder's pre-amplifier with some advantage and its performance when subject to very large signals is unimportant. Such a design is shown in Fig. 14. For use with some recorders the output of this circuit may be too high to make the signal respond adequately to the gain control and its gain may be reduced by substituting a higher value resistor for the 330 ohm value shown. Reducing the gain of the pre-amplifier in this way will reduce still further the already low noise. Another design of pre-amplifier is shown in Fig. 15. This one is slightly inferior in noise level but incorporates a bass cut filter which can be useful in reducing unwanted low-frequency mechanical noise. Both these designs are arranged for balanced microphone leads and are suitable for medium and low impedance microphones using long leads when required.

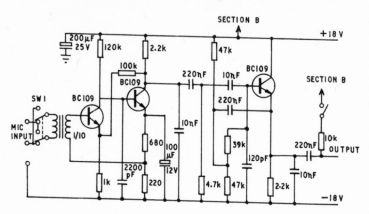

Fig. 15 Low-noise microphone amplifier with 125 Hz 24 dB/octave filter

As noted in Chapter 4, the majority of recorders do not permit a direct line input but are arranged so that all inputs find their way through the recorder's own pre-amplifier, those at high level being attenuated to avoid overloading.

If a microphone pre-amplifier is connected between the microphone and any of these inputs so that the actual signal applied to the recorder's pre-amplifier is higher than if the microphone had been directly connected, then at first glance it may be thought that this is bound to produce a better signal-to-noise ratio at the record amplifier input. However, this overlooks the fact that the noise produced by the microphone pre-amplifier, albeit quite low compared with the signal, will now be subject to the recorder's own pre-amplifier high gain. Thus the combined signal at the gain control will contain even more noise than if the microphone had been directly connected. The increase in gain in the wanted signal may, however, be sufficient to ensure that there is an improved signal-to-noise ratio.

Whether there will be any improvement depends on the relative noise levels of the microphone pre-amplifier and the recorder's pre-amplifier and on how they are connected. To succeed, the microphone pre-amplifier must be significantly quieter and if possible the microphone pre-amplifier should be connected directly to the recorder's pre-amplifier without any attenuation.

There is little doubt that either of the two designs shown in Figs 14 and 15 will improve the performance of the more modest cassette recorders.

HEADPHONES AND EARPIECES

The use of headphones and earpieces has been referred to in connection with monitoring the signal either before or after it has been recorded. The quality of such equipment must be good if the sound being heard with them is being used as a form of control. In particular they must have a frequency response capable of covering the repertoire of the species recorded.

There are many good earphones available with satisfactory frequency response, and after checking that they are of the correct impedance, the only remaining considerations are whether they will be comfortable to wear and easy to carry.

Many headphones resemble pudding bowls and are both bulky and uncomfortable to wear outdoors in hot weather. They may be ideal for use at home by the fireside so that the user may exclude all other sounds, but this is unnecessary for our purpose. The type that rest on the surface of the ear are quite adequate, are lighter and less bulky, and can be removed with one hand without causing noise or discomfort.

TRIPODS

The only other item that may be needed is a tripod to support the reflector. Modern camera tripods are usually quite adequate even though the weight of microphone and reflector probably exceeds the weight of any camera for which they were designed. For camera work the tripod has to be free of vibration which means that its construction is usually adequate for holding a reflector.

Camera tripods usually incorporate a pan and tilt head which is very useful in setting up a reflector, but of course cannot be used during actual recording without causing handling noise.

BINOCULARS

Binoculars are an extra luxury that adds immeasurably to the enjoyment of an expedition, and they are often vital in making a visual identification. Suitable binoculars for bird watching usually have a magnification of seven to eight times. It is generally found that binoculars with a bigger magnification than this cannot be held steady. The diameter of the objective lens governs the amount of light admitted and the larger the lens the brighter the image seen. The diameter also governs the width of the field of vision and is specified in millimetres. Thus binoculars in common use are specified as 7×40, 7×50, 8×50, or 8×60. The latter size have such large objective lens that they are often called night glasses. Binoculars to these specifications are heavy and require both hands to hold them up to the eyes. Binoculars 6×30 are by contrast very light and can be used with one hand. Although not used for normal bird watching they are quite adequate for identifying species within normal recording distance.

CLOTHING, ETC.

It may seem strange that clothing comes under review but a few hints and tips may help to avoid a wrong purchase. The recordist's hands are usually full of equipment so it is essential that the garments worn give adequate protection without the necessity for constant changing. Any surplus clothing interferes with mobility and is a constant source of annoyance.

A top coat should be large enough to accommodate several layers of clothing which can be varied to suit the season and time of day – a greenish gabardine coat to blend well with the outdoors, front opening with adequate pockets, detachable hood and perhaps detachable fur lining would be suitable. The pockets should be large enough to accommodate a few spools of tape, spare batteries and leads, gloves and a torch, together with any other items required. Beware of nylon coats which rustle with the least movement of the body. These rustlings will be faithfully reproduced on your recordings!

Gloves or mittens are a must for winter and early morning sessions and should be chosen so that the recorder's controls can be operated whilst wearing them.

Footwear depends to some extent on the type of habitat and is a personal choice. The main hazards are squeaky boots and nailed boots, both of which will announce your coming to all and sundry, not to mention your intended recording subject.

Emergency food rations are a matter of choice. However, the hobby is very absorbing and time passes so quickly that it is often possible for the dedicated recordist to discover during a lull in recording that he is very hungry. A glance at his watch confirms that it is many hours since he has eaten and it is then that the odd biscuit or chocolate bar can save the day for many more hours of pleasant recording.

7

Field Techniques

INTRODUCTION

This chapter deals with the use of equipment in the field and is mainly devoted to recording in mono. The variations to adapt these techniques to stereo recording are dealt with in Chapter 8.

Some of the techniques described must be applied with care to avoid disturbance to wildlife. Fortunately an increasing number of species are now legally protected and even those still not covered are deserving of consideration. Birds can easily be disturbed during the nesting season, often quite accidentally.

MICROPHONE TECHNIQUES

REFLECTOR

The reflector enables recordings to be made with very little preparation, and causes no disturbance to the subject, while its keen directional property enables the recordist to single out any individual almost to the exclusion of others. It also has the advantage of allowing recording at a much greater distance than when using an open microphone.

The most popular method of using a reflector is to hand-hold the device, usually in the right hand. The left hand is then free to manipulate the recorder slung over the left shoulder. This method enables the recordist to move himself and equipment quickly and quietly but has some disadvantages. The combined weight of microphone and reflector can cause arm fatigue and handling noise ensues. Handling noise is caused by vibrations being transmitted to the microphone and recorded at the same time as the wanted sound. In wildlife sound recording, the signal is often weak and requires a high gain setting. This results in the handling noise being greatly amplified and it may even exceed the wanted sound. With continual use the arm becomes accustomed to the weight but it is vitally important that the reflector should have a comfortable handle and that the assembly should be well balanced. A further disadvantage is that the microphone is uncomfortably close to the recorder and, in consequence, the microphone can easily pick up mechanical noise from the machine. It is therefore essential to keep the two items as far apart as possible. In practice this is done by making sure that the recorder is slightly to the rear of the left hip. Unfortunately, in this position, it is often difficult to see the VU meter and the recorder must be operated more by feel.

The hand-held reflector makes many types of recording possible. Birds that sing best in flight are one example; skylarks and woodlarks seldom sing well on the ground. Keeping an accurate aim on a moving subject will not be found easy without creating handling noise, particularly if the reflector is tilted and mechanically unbalanced. Care must be taken to ensure that the microphone lead is securely fastened and will not grate against the edge of the reflector as it is panned.

A minor though not insignificant advantage of using a reflector is the wind protection that it affords to the microphone.

If in spite of using a lightweight reflector the weight is still found to be unmanageable, some relief can be obtained by resorting to a monopod. A monopod can be devised simply and cheaply from a broom handle. One end is securely attached to the reflector and the other end rests

on the ground, thereby taking the weight otherwise supported by the arm. On gravel paths it is better to rest the
monopod on the toe of the shoe so that the noise transmitted up the monopod is reduced. The monopod thus still
enables the user to maintain mobility.

A third method of using a reflector is to mount it on a
tripod. Instant mobility is thereby destroyed but it does
enable the recordist to site his recorder well away from the
reflector. Pan and tilt heads are useful to set up the
reflector but cannot be used during actual recording.
Provided the subject is stationary, the use of a tripod can
be recommended. A suitable subject would be a nesting
colony of gulls on a cliff face, recorded at some distance.
With such a subject it is impossible to single out any
individual bird and therefore there is no need to move the
reflector during recording. On the other hand, the chances
of making satisfactory recordings of many of our warblers
with a tripod-mounted reflector are very slim as such
subjects seldom remain perched for any length of time.
Recorded from a distance of thirteen metres or less a movement of only two metres is sufficient to require the reflector
to be re-aimed or there will be a severe loss in signal
strength.

GUN MICROPHONES

A gun microphone of the capacitor type is sufficiently
sensitive to allow it to be used in exactly the same manner
as a reflector-mounted microphone and it is not so cumber-
some. It is less directional than the reflector and easier to
aim, and sounds recorded include species singing adjacent
to the main subject.

It has already been shown that the capacitor gun microphone is superior to the reflector in frequency response,
no matter how good the quality of the microphone in the
reflector. This is particularly true at the lower end of the
audio spectrum, so the use of a gun microphone to record

species whose voices contain low frequencies should produce more faithful recordings. Its wider angle of acceptance makes the microphone more suitable than the reflector for recording atmospheres.

OPEN MICROPHONES

While this term might be applied to gun microphones it usually refers to the use of an ordinary omni-directional or cardioid microphone without a reflector.

Some experienced recordists will not use a microphone in a reflector as they claim it distorts the sound, but the chances of making a good recording with the same microphone held in the hand are not very good as it is unlikely that the subject will be in suitable range. For recording bird song, therefore, it is better to try the open microphone technique using long leads.

In the breeding season many birds have their favourite song posts and if a microphone is placed near to each post the chances of making a good recording are considerably enhanced. A useful gadget for such an occasion is a box into which all the microphone inputs are fed and a switch so that any one can be selected to give an output to the recorder. It is then possible to wait, maybe in the comfort of a car. If the subject can be seen, switch to the nearest microphone and if the signal is satisfactory release the pause button of the recorder. If the subject cannot be seen, random switching to find the most favoured microphone can be used.

Occasionally the bird can sing so closely to the microphone that the gain must be very much reduced to avoid over-modulation. This reduces the ambience to a mere whisper, resulting in a sound you might hear if the bird could be induced to sing sitting on your shoulder. This makes the recording sound a little unreal.

Insects, amphibians and nestlings can be approached more easily and there should be no difficulty in obtaining a strong enough signal with an open microphone. A useful aid for this purpose is a broom handle, in fact even several broom handles joined together with metal sleeves, to the end of which the microphone is firmly secured. The whole assembly can then be raised so that the microphone is only inches away from the subject.

It is better to record insects in temporary captivity to avoid ambient noises which will drown their relatively low-strength signals.

REFLECTOR, GUN MICROPHONE OR OPEN MICROPHONE?

The novice should have an open mind on which technique to use. For general work a reflector or gun microphone will give more satisfaction, but the possibility of using open microphone technique should not be ignored.

For a general early-morning expedition with nothing specific in mind, the recordist may well content himself with the reflector or gun microphone technique. This may lead to the discovery of a nest which can lead to a further expedition for the purpose of recording feeding sequences etc. If it is possible to place an open microphone close to the nest without disturbance, this is the technique to use. This will often mean a long wait between any signals suitable for recording.

OMNI OR CARDIOID?

The omni-directional microphone used in open fashion is suitable for recording atmosphere. Since the object is to collect sound from all directions the microphone should be pointed vertically upwards; given the right conditions, it could be hand-held in this position. Although classed as omni-directional, it will have a somewhat reduced sensitivity to sounds reaching it from the rear. As the rear will point to the ground, from which, presumably, no sound will be emanating, it will thus be best placed to receive all other wanted sounds.

For recording insects, amphibians, reptiles, etc. where the microphone can be held close to the subject, a cardioid microphone would be the better choice as it will assist in excluding unwanted sounds.

The type of microphone to use in a reflector is not at once obvious. A reflector converts an omni-directional microphone into a highly directional instrument, so what purpose can be served by using a cardioid microphone, which is highly directional, in a reflector? The response curves in Chapter 5 indicate that the reflector gives less gain at low frequencies when a cardioid microphone is in use. This arrangement, therefore, acts as a bass cut filter and helps in cutting out unwanted low-frequency sounds. On the other hand, if the subject is also a source of low frequencies it would be much better to use an omni-directional microphone.

This therefore indicates that the choice of microphone to be used in a reflector is dictated by the frequency range of the subject to be recorded. In general the omni-directional microphone will give the best frequency response but the advantage of the bass-cut characteristics of the cardioid should not be overlooked.

THE USE OF A MAINS MACHINE

Some years ago very few portables could equal the performance of a mains machine. Professional recordings were generally made on mains machines, relying on long microphone leads to maintain some semblance of mobility. To overcome the mains problem a DC/AC inverter powered from a car battery was used. In fact the car became a mobile studio giving power and accommodation. Modern portables will satisfy the most fastidious user and this technique is now practically obsolete.

However, there are many who initially only possess a mains machine and there is no reason why they should not adopt this technique as a temporary expedient. The inverter mentioned is an expensive item of equipment and it is therefore recommended that the method should be used only within reach of a mains supply. Most gardens can provide a lot of useful material throughout the year.

The safest way is to employ long microphone leads, keeping the mains leads short. Trailing AC cables on damp ground can be lethal! Open microphones may be used or even a reflector if an assistant is available. Failing the help of an assistant, some recorders can be stopped and started remotely. The author made his first wildlife sound recording in this way and the method is still used occasionally.

MONITORING

Monitoring means listening to the signal as received through the microphone and recorder, usually over headphones. On the best machines the signal may be heard before or after it is recorded and it is therefore possible to check the quality of the recording as it is being made. If the signal can only be heard before it is recorded, it is necessary to rely on the reading of the VU meter and judge a suitable setting for the gain control. In this instance monitoring provides confirmation that the signal is suitable for recording. When the first method can be used, the recordist need not refer to the VU meter at all during recording, and this is a distinct advantage when concentrating on the movements of his subject.

Without headphones a reflector must be aimed using the peephole, but with headphones the reflector can be aimed using the ears as a guide. Both methods are employed, either separately or simultaneously as conditions dictate. Sometimes it is possible to keep the reflector out of the wind by holding it low down where it would be difficult to use the peephole, and headphones can then be used. At times when it is dark the subject cannot be seen and if the VU meter cannot be illuminated by a built-in lamp or a torch, headphones are essential in aiming the reflector. In any case the use of lights may cause disturbance. The use of headphones when recording a subject that may move unexpectedly in any direction is unlikely to be successful. The purely visual method enables the reflector to be panned and re-aimed more quickly and accurately.

Thus monitoring with headphones when using a reflector can be of considerable assistance under certain conditions and in others might even be considered a hindrance. Headphones are certainly not essential and the novice may well be advised not to use them until he has gained experience.

When using open microphone technique, however, headphones are useful. With this method the microphone is often remote from the recordist and only the headphones can tell if the signal being received is worth recording. However, if the recordist is far enough away and sufficiently sound-insulated from the microphone, he can dispense with headphones altogether and monitor over the recorder's own loudspeaker.

THE USE OF A HIDE

Even with reasonably long microphone leads, whether connected to an open microphone or to a reflector pre-trained on some specific point, concealment may often still be necessary. Hiding behind a bush or a wall or some other suitable handy object may well suffice, but the complete absence of such features calls for the use of a tent hide. One of the most convenient hides for a recordist, and also the most comfortable, is a car. It is a fairly well-known fact that it is the outline of man which is most disturbing, and very little attention is paid to an occupied car. Thus the car gives nearly perfect visibility and an almost perfect hide.

CALL DOWN

Most naturalists agree that bird song is used to proclaim and defend territorial rights. It is only natural, therefore, that a bird on hearing a sound recording of his song is tempted to investigate and sing with extra vigour. There is thus a temptation to replay tapes in the field in the hope that this will happen, when a further recording can be made at a more suitable distance.

The full meaning of many calls is still not understood and in accordance with the type of recording chosen the subject may either disappear in complete silence, become very agitated and attack the recordist or the recorder, or even desert a nest which is then subject to predation or the nestlings to chilling. If the call down continues it is quite possible for a bird to a desert the territory completely.

For these reasons the technique is not recommended. There may be exceptional cases when call down is permissible but great care should be taken not to cause distress and the recordist should certainly have some knowledge of the effect the call is likely to have on the bird.

INITIAL EXPERIMENTS

The relative difficulties in taking up the hobby of wildlife sound recording are debatable but the transition from general recording appears to be easier than the transition from naturalist to recordist. However, there are always exceptions to any general rule.

Provided the subject to be recorded can be found without difficulty, the general recordist will need little initial advice on how to operate the equipment. Depending on previous experience, however, the unpredictable performance of his subject and the apparent weak strength of the signal will be frustrating. The experienced naturalist may be less frustrated by the behaviour of the subject but will accept a much lower signal strength than desirable. Initially the general recordist will probably have some difficulty in identifying the species recorded, but the first objective should be to make good recordings, leaving identification for later.

There is a saying that there are three kinds of bird watchers – the bird-table watcher, the go-anywhere bird watcher, and the ornithologist. To these I would add a fourth – the wildlife sound recordist.

Once the general recordist starts wildlife sound recording he will inevitably become a bird watcher as well. Joining a bird class or a local bird group will help with problems of identification. A number of good books are also available and these often attempt to give an indication of the song in words. There are also a number of discs which can assist. In this manner the general recordist can learn how to identify recordings and where to find suitable subjects.

The experienced naturalist will have to learn that the habitats in which he has already devoted many patient hours to observing birds may be entirely unsuitable for recording. The right habitat must be free from mechanical noise and relatively free from human visitation. To some extent these conditions can be met by choosing the right time of day to record. A habitat may be ideal at 6 o'clock in the morning but absolutely impossible two hours later. In some circumstances, the noise of trains, traffic and aircraft may be present continuously. Therefore, a habitat near a busy main-line railway, a motorway or a major airport would be unsuitable at any time.

FIRST STEPS

Before attempting to record wildlife sound the novice should spend some time familiarizing himself with his equipment. He must practise operating the recorder until its use becomes instinctive. This will avoid fumbling at some critical moment when any error could result in the complete loss of a good recording.

To gain experience, recordings can be made in the garden even though the surroundings may be very noisy. On replay the novice will be shocked to find that he has recorded sounds of distant traffic, aircraft, children playing and dogs barking up to half a mile away, none of which was noticed at the time of recording. The average person tends to hear a single activity and doesn't notice other unwanted sounds. Only when the single activity becomes inaudible owing to the presence of other sounds does he complain about noise.

The recordist, however, becomes accustomed to listening for background noise that will be recorded at the same time as the chosen subject and can decide in advance whether the amount of unwanted noise will be acceptable to him on playback. The decision depends on what standard of recording it is hoped to achieve. Some noise can be practically eliminated by filtering in the studio, as we shall see in a later chapter. Indeed, some recordists may filter the sound while recording.

Another object of practising at home is to learn how easily noise created by the recordist can be transferred physically to the microphone. This will show how essential it is to use an anti-vibration mount such as is described in Chapter 2. However, even with this precaution, the microphone must be handled with care.

When the microphone is mounted in a reflector and the reflector is hand-held, problems due to the size of the reflector can arise. In a tight thicket it is all too easy to find that the edge of the reflector has been rubbing against twigs which again produce handling noise. Even a gentle breeze blowing blades of grass against the reflector or rain dropping can have the same effect.

Do not miss an opportunity to experiment during windy weather. No windshield is perfect. Severe buffeting will register on the VU meter but milder buffeting only becomes apparent when the recording is replayed in quiet surroundings. Experiments may be carried out facing the wind, back to the wind, etc., each time dictating a message explaining the circumstances of the recording. In this way it will be discovered how much wind can be tolerated.

Having built or acquired the best windshield possible it is advisable to use it at all times since gusts of wind can spring up unexpectedly. In exposed places it may be necessary to seek additional shelter. Experiments will have shown that the direction of the wind is important. Wind buffeting on the microphone produces distortion, but the sound of wind in nearby reeds, trees, etc. assists in setting the scene. This effect is more acceptable in stereo. Mono recordings that include wind are not so convincing and many would prefer the same recording made on a still day.

Very often at dusk and dawn the wind drops completely or is not so strong. This points yet again to the early hours being the best ones for field work.

By this time some dexterity of operation will have been acquired. If the recorder is key-operated the recordist must learn how to use the keys quietly. At some stage it could be necessary to use stalking technique and it is point-less to gain a suitable recording position only to disturb the subject by heavy key operation. Playback howl, which is caused by putting the recorder into the record mode while its internal speaker is switched on, will probably also have been experienced. Imagine the effect this would have on the chosen subject!

EVALUATING RECORDINGS

During these experiments recordings of blackbirds and robins, which are two good subjects, will probably have been attempted. Finding the birds will present no problem and they are so tame that approach should be easy. Their songs are of different character and frequency range, and making good recordings should give excellent experience.

The blackbird song is strong and clear and its upper frequencies can be captured with relatively cheap microphones. Very satisfactory recordings can be made using a reflector at anything up to thirty-five metres distance. Time spent recording a blackbird is far from time wasted in terms of experience gained, and when the recordings are heard it will be apparent that some of them are much better than others. If adequate notes were made during recording it will be obvious which is the best way to make improvements. Recording notes can be dictated so that they are heard directly after each recording. Try to note the distance, the gain setting on the recorder, how the VU meter behaved, whether the subject was facing the recordist, etc. Compare the results and note how some recordings are clearer and more distinct than others. If during recording the VU meter often swung over into the red, the recording will be over-modulated. Recognizing over-modulation distortion by ear is not easy, but once this form of distortion is recognized the recordist is a long way on the path to producing good recordings. Recordings made at the shortest distance without over-modulation will appear to be the best, particularly if the subject is facing the recordist. In this position the gain on the recorder will be comparatively low, producing a better signal-to-noise ratio. In addition, the strength of the desired signal relative to the ambient noise will be much better. If the subject is facing the recordist there will be added clarity to the song.

Recording the robin presents different problems. Compared to the blackbird the song appears weak and is of much higher frequency. First attempts are almost certain to produce over-modulated recordings and yet the VU meter will have registered a much lower reading than it did when successfully recording the blackbird. The answer to this lies in the response time of the VU meter. The robin, in common with the wren and numerous other birds, is capable of producing bursts of song of high intensity but of such short duration that the VU meter does not have time to register them before the burst is finished. But the electronics respond and pass on a signal to the tape, and the result is over-modulation. Detecting over-modulation of robin song by ear is again much more difficult than in the case of the blackbird. The song's characteristics, particularly the high-frequency notes, sound very similar to an over-modulation and only critical comparison between the original song and the recording will eventually show the recordist whether he has achieved the desired result.

The problem of over-modulation is one that will trouble the recordist a great deal. First attempts at recording the robin will show the limitations of the VU meter. The object should always be to produce a fully modulated tape, but there is a grave danger of over-modulation if the subject is too near. Experience in setting the gain control to its correct position is gained by trial and error.

After some experience the recordist will venture further afield and opportunities for applying different techniques will present themselves. If there is any doubt as to which microphone technique should be applied, why not try a number? The results can be compared and further experience gained.

Further reading

PETERSON, R., MOUNTFORD, G. and HOLLOM, P.A.D., *A*

Field Guide to the Birds of Britain and Europe, 3rd edition, Collins, 1974.

Royal Society for the Protection of Birds, *Wild Birds and the Law*.

STEPHEN, C., *A Guide to Watching Wildlife*, Collins, 1973.

8

Stereo Wildlife Sound Recording

INTRODUCTION

For some fifteen years, music lovers have been able to reproduce their favourite disc recordings in stereo. Devotees claim that the added dimension adds immeasurably to their pleasure.

Hi-fi, a term originally employed for high-quality reproduction of sound in mono form, could not now be claimed for a system restricted to mono, although stereo reproduction alone cannot be regarded as hi-fi. To merit this title, both the channels constituting a stereo system must be every bit as good as the single channel formerly used for mono, and the two channels must match each other as nearly as possible.

Thus the equipment required in the home to do full justice to the material available on disc is not likely to be cheap. Even with unlimited equipment resources, adequate space is required in the living room which in itself should present a symmetrical acoustic load to the carefully matched speakers. The loudspeakers must be located correctly and orientated in a proper manner. Advice on all these problems has been handed out *ad nauseam* in various hi-fi publications, but it is true to say that only when all the conditions are met can a real stereophonic impression be created, and even then only over a very limited area.

Those fortunate enough to have experienced the effect and having established a really good system may well be tempted to ask why they should not record wildlife sounds in stereo. It is a good question and one worthy of a considered reply.

At the outset it will be readily appreciated that field equipment is going to be more expensive. Portable stereo recorders are obviously going to cost considerably more than their mono counterparts. In addition two microphones will be required. As the cost of equipment is higher than for mono and is considerably more difficult to use, we should perhaps first attempt to answer the question usually asked – is it worth while?

Again, there is no straightforward answer as it all depends on the type of recording. If, for a moment, I can refer once more to music reproduction, it cannot be denied that some subjects are better than others, even when due allowance is made for the varying degrees of skill of recordists and the acoustics of studios. A piece of music such as a concerto in which a soloist is given prominence is not so effective as a small ensemble. In fact, chamber music, specifically named because the musicians can be accommodated in a small room, when reproduced stereophonically in the home is the perfect subject.

In wildlife recording of a single species we have the equivalent of the concerto, and recorded in stereo it is not as effective as a dawn chorus. Continuing the analogy, the dawn chorus corresponds to the small ensemble. A fairly distant recording of a gull colony compares with a symphony where the effect is reasonable but not comparable to the dawn chorus. In general, therefore, stereo wildlife recordings are probably at their best for reasonably close-up atmosphere recordings.

Many may disagree with this summary. Wildlife stereo recording is still in its infancy and not many recordists are wholly committed to such work. Some recordists regard it as a waste of time for recording solo species and its value for scientific and record purposes is doubtful.

In spite of the foregoing there are a growing number of

recordists who, while not being wholly committed, are now regularly working in stereo. Therefore if the beginner wishes to venture into this realm, some practical advice will not come amiss.

STEREO MICROPHONE TECHNIQUES

Apart from the duplication of equipment the first obvious difference is that during recording microphones must not be moved, or at least the consequence of movement must be quickly assessed in advance, otherwise the ultimate listener can be treated to a dizzy reeling effect.

Perhaps the greatest difficulty in stereo recording is the choice of microphone technique. Our ears are omni-directional and we are able to enjoy stereophonic sound naturally, owing to the slight time delay in sound arriving from any given point at each ear. First attempts at stereo-phonic recording in the studio were made by placing two omni-directional microphones one on each side of a dummy head. It was thought that the deflection of sound by the model head might well have a bearing on the quality of the stereophony achieved.

However, the result turned out to be greatly inferior to that expected, presumably because the brain is much more efficient at differentiating the time delay than our micro-phones. To compensate for this the spacing was increased and it was found that the greater the distance apart, the better the stereophonic effect. However, with such wide spacing, sounds from the extreme right or left arrive so much later at the farther microphone that the result is a quick flutter echo. When applied to wildlife recording, if a bird flies by on a parallel path closer to the microphones than their distance apart, the result is a volume dip as the bird passes the mid-point. Nevertheless, many successful wildlife recordings have been made using this method,

(*Above*) The starling – a bird which repays recording by the variety and unpredictability of its calls and mimicry. (*Photo:* Ardea London)

(*Below*) The common toad – its soft call presents a challenge to the recordist. (*Photo:* John Marchington, Ardea London)

The grey squirrel – a suggested subject for study.

Recording insects. The insects are enclosed in a sound-proof chamber and observed through a glass window. A lamp provides illumination and warms the chamber. The recorder is a Nagra III. (*Photo:* Jack Skeel)

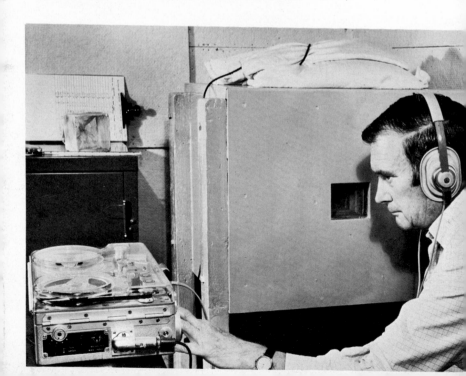

but for the reasons given the results cannot be claimed to be consistent.

One method of reducing the defects is to use a relatively large sheet of sound-insulating material between micro-phones only a few inches apart. The object, of course, is to artificially create a time delay between the signals arriving at each microphone.

In recording studios good results were obtained by using a pair of cardioid microphones mounted one above the other with their axes inclined at an angle depending on the shape of the cardioid characteristic. Generally an angle of about 60° was found to be best. Too small an angle results in a reduced width of sound stage and loss of stereo effect, while too large an angle produces no sound from the centre, often referred to as a 'hole in the middle'. On the whole, this technique produces more consistent results than open omni-directional microphones and is recom-mended for atmosphere recording.

All the problems associated with using open micro-phones for mono recording apply to stereo recording, and there is the added problem of obtaining balance. All too often more sound originates from one side than from the other and the microphone pair must be rotated until the dividing axis of the pair points to the centre of greatest sound activity. If the microphones are connected by long leads, visiting them to adjust their direction can disturb the subject being recorded – thus we create a vicious circle.

If two cardioid microphones are capable of producing good stereo, why not the use of two reflector-mounted microphones? It could be argued that the improved signal strength would enable the recordist to stand by the re-flectors and adjust them at will without disturbing the subject.

David J. Tombs carried out a number of experiments with two reflector-mounted microphones and found that

E

when the two were close together there was little sound produced from the centre. When mounted farther apart the same flutter echo occurred as with open microphones. Accordingly he concluded that the use of two reflectors could not be recommended.

Sten Wahlstrom, as long ago as April 1969, recommended the use of a split or divided reflector. Basically this consisted of a vertical barrier placed in a single reflector and one microphone located at each side. As this means that neither microphone can be located at the exact focal point, they are set back a little and inclined at an angle to the partition, with the idea that the partition acts as a second reflector. Thus the axis of the microphone should be arranged to intercept the reflector at the focal point. The effect is enhanced if cardioid microphones are used.

David Tombs repeated this method and found it produced very good results, particularly for distant recording where the angle of the sound stage is likely to be small. Sounds more than 10° either side of the axis fall off very rapidly.

In an effort to improve the width of the sound stage some recordists have constructed special reflectors made in two separate halves. Each half is slightly wider than half the width of a normal reflector, so that the microphone head can be accurately located at the focal point. Finally the two halves are bolted together so that the axes of each half are inclined outwards to each other at an angle of about 5°.

As capacitor gun microphones have much greater sensitivity than dynamic microphones, a pair can be used in place of the split reflector. The pair are mounted on a suitable bracket inclined outwards to each other at an angle of about 30°. As they are not so highly directional as reflector-mounted microphones they give a better spread of sound and are very much favoured for fairly close recording work such as warblers in a woodland setting. The only drawback is the rather high cost.

FIELD CHECKS

When setting up microphones for stereo recording it is important that their electrical outputs shall be in phase. Most hi-fi enthusiasts know the importance of making sure that stereo loudspeakers are phased so that their diaphragms are operating in the same direction at any given moment. Incorrectly phased loudspeakers produce a sound-cancelling effect. If the loudspeakers are correctly phased but the microphone outputs are not similarly in phase, the sound-cancelling effect will occur on playback.

With the use of extension leads, microphone preamplifiers, etc. there is always a possibility that the connections will have been reversed, so before any recording is attempted a phase check should be made. Microphone preamplifiers usually have a means of paralleling the two microphones on to one channel, and a phase reversing switch is incorporated on one of the two microphone inputs. With the two microphones paralleled the reversing switch can be operated and the position which gives the higher VU reading is obviously the correct one. Instead of the VU meter the headphones may be used to determine which position of the switch results in the louder signal.

PRODUCTION OF STEREO RECORDINGS

Very few recording studios now restrict themselves to the use of two microphones. Generally multi-track recorders are used and the individual artists perform in complete isolation from other members of the same group, receiving their cues from each other by headphones. Thus each artist's contribution is recorded completely independently and the combination of all these recordings into two channels is the creative work of the sound mixer, who starts his work when all recording is finished. This rather artificial procedure is carried to extremes in the case of 'pop' recording where the recordist can add reverberation or other effects to individual recordings and can mix the recordings in any manner he chooses. The final result probably even surprises the artists.

Multi-track recording technique could be applied to wildlife sound recording if it were possible to produce suitable portables.

However, we are fortunate that our birds are all individualists and their performances are usually unrelated, so there seems no reason why multi-track techniques should not be used, even if the individual tracks are recorded at different times and at different localities. Indeed, a stereo stage could be created using entirely mono recordings. The ethics of such a creation are perhaps open to question, but if we accept that stereo recording is merely to create an illusion, the means by which it is achieved are of no consequence.

The addition of a stereo background to a mono recording of a single species is worth experiment. If the mono recording includes very little else but the voice of a single species it can be made to move at the same time as the stereo background is added. Of course, care must be taken that the end product does not create an impossible situation by including different species that are never known to be found together. Again any movements must be natural. For example, birds that do not sing on the wing must not be made to do so electronically.

Thus the techniques and equipment are available, and it is merely a question of applying them correctly. The author has experimented on all these lines and is perfectly satisfied that an illusion of stereo can be created electronically that is indistinguishable from recordings made in stereo in the field. The method has much to commend it, because once the basic recordings are made, their combination into a simulated stereo programme lies within the complete control of the recordist.

THE FUTURE

Quadrophony has recently been introduced into the domestic hi-fi field and once again the addicts are claiming that no system can be truly hi-fi without this further added dimension. With it the listener can be persuaded that he is actually seated in the middle of the orchestra, although its real purpose is to recreate the echoes from the rear of the hall.

For wildlife recording the technique could be used to transport the listener to the heart of a wood and might be very effective. Its use for recording a cliff colony of gulls where there is little sound from the rear would probably effect no improvement. For the present, although there are four-track (recording on all tracks simultaneously) mains machines available, there are no portable counterparts and it is problematical as to when such recordings will be possible.

The latest innovation is ambisonic recording. Conventional stereo creates a line image of sound, i.e. sounds appear to emanate anywhere from a line joining the two loudspeakers. Quadraphonic sound creates a plane image, sounds emanating from all directions but strictly in a horizontal plane created by the four loudspeakers. Ambisonic sound attempts to recreate sounds from all directions.

It is curious to note that the method used for ambisonic recording goes back to the old dummy head system. If the recording is played back over the usual conventional stereo twin speaker set-up, the results are disappointing, the main complaint being a hole in the middle. However, if the recording is played back direct into the ears using good-quality headphones, the result is claimed to surpass anything achieved so far with conventional stereo or quadrophonic equipment. It is interesting to note that recordings made expressly for replaying over stereo equipment, when listened to with headphones, produce sounds apparently originating inside the head, but with true dummy head recording this defect does not exist. If good-quality headphones had been available at reasonable prices some twenty years ago, perhaps stereo as we generally accept it would never have become so popular. One main defect in ambisonic recording is that it is even more anti-social than our conventional stereo set-up. At least with conventional stereo two or three people can be treated to an illusion of stereo and be aware that they are all listening to the same programme.

The success of the system depends on the construction of the dummy head, details of which are a closely guarded secret of the recording studios. Sufficient is known to suggest that making one to studio standards is beyond most amateur resources. However, one microphone manufacturer has produced a pair of microphones to be worn like a stethoscope so that the recordist uses his own head, and it is probably the use of this type of equipment that offers the wildlife sound recordist scope for experiment.

Further reading

TOMBS, D. J., 'Wildlife Recording in Stereo', *Journal of the British Institute of Recorded Sound*, No. 54, April 1974.

9

Some Bird Sounds of Possible Interest

by Alan Mitchell

One of the commonest and most ubiquitous birds to record is the STARLING. This bird repays recording by the variety and unpredictability of its calls and its mimicry. A contact-call is a clear descending whistle often followed by a high-pitched whickering. In one locality in north-east London, and doubtless elsewhere, the local garden population had a regular 'question and response' system. One bird would make a short, rising clear whistle, 'phawee', and all others within range would cry out 'catchet'. In the air the contact-call is a harsh bubbling note, and a stronger version of this, something like 'skrrrridge', is used on taking off, perhaps a combination of contact and mild alarm, but the true alarm is a very sharp 'twik'. This note is rarely, if ever, mis-used and promotes instant evasive action and a dive for cover. It is the standard note for the appearance of a sparrowhawk and has twice enabled me to see one from my garden.

When singing, the bird is usually in a prominent position, a chimney-pot, television aerial or dead top of a tree, and it may sing at any time of day or year. The effort is considerable, entailing straining so far forward that the wings have to make partial flaps to preserve the balance. The bill opens widely and the throat bulges and palpitates.

It seems as if the sounds have to be brought up from a great depth, since for all this hard work little that emerges has much carrying power or body. Much quiet wuzzling and scratching is interspersed with whirrs, clicks and whistles. However, every starling seems to be equipped with three items of pure mimicry. Few sing long without a descending 'wick-wick-wick-wick' and this is the song of the lesser spotted woodpecker rather carelessly performed. The inevitable 'churruck' call of the moorhen and the 'chizzick' flight-note of the pied wagtail are, however, very well done. By estuaries most starlings add the warning call 'tee-yoo-too-too' of the redshank, and some the 'tulee' of the ringed plover.

The point here is that there may be any number of local variants both in mimicry (which are also sometimes highly individual, some surprising ones being reported, like the learning of a milkman's old-fashioned yodel) and in tricks like the call and response. There is much to be learned in the alarm-calls of different meaning, the details of the normal song and its variants and whether there exist well-marked dialects. The winter visitors which swarm in from Scandinavia and Eastern Europe may emit mimicry of species familiar to them at nesting time. The second-rate mimicry of the lesser spotted woodpecker may be replaced by a better one of the green woodpecker by some birds. The field for discoveries is wide.

The starling turns everything to its own account, being a highly intelligent, resourceful bird which, not being adapted to any specialized feeding or other habit, has become a general-purpose bird able to exploit almost anything. It is a strong flier, a strong, if decidedly plodding, walker and it has a strong, sharp bill, ideal as a general-purpose tool and prodder. It may be found anywhere, from the centres of the largest cities, where it forms spectacular mass roosts, to the wildest mountain tops where it will appear for the hatch of tiny beetles and flies, and to

marshes and saltings where winter immigrants tend to
flock. Suburban gardens are a stronghold of the resident
birds, and in urban woodlands or in woods overtaken by
the spread of industry it is starlings that inherit all the
woodpecker holes. Even among factories and in busy railway goods yards there will be starlings if there is any tip-
ping of rubbish or any weedy land around. Rich farmlands
have them among the cattle; young conifer plantations on
moorland may suffer extensive damage from their roosting;
lake and reservoir banks attract them – nowhere is long
without starlings.

The WOODLARK has a song as beautiful as any and more
sustained probably than any other. A tape with ten
minutes' song on it would be a fine possession and a joy
to play. The song is delivered as the bird circles in a lazy
dipping flight some three hundred feet or more above the
ground. The song is a long series of phrases with scarcely
a pause between, each one of similar pattern but with great
variation in detail. The voice has that light clarity and
purity which gives rise to the adjective 'silvery' and the
song carries well. A typical phrase is a somewhat stuttering
opening, rising and gaining in confidence, 'chik-chok-
chik-chip-chipchip...' holding at the top and becoming
silvery and fluent then cascading down 'tloo-tloo-looloo-
loolooloo...' dying away in a yodelling then immediately
starting the next one. To hear this pouring softly down
from a moonlit sky at midnight for a solid hour is a memor-
able experience. The woodlark may sing at any time of
year from the last days of December until about July, but
it does need a calm sunny day, at least in the early part
of the year. It sings most around sunrise, but if the day
is right it will be heard freely until midday, less in the
afternoon, probably little in the evening, but sometimes
it will start again well after dark and may be singing at
four in the morning if dawn is not imminent.

The woodlark is a southern bird and displays big cyclic

changes in numbers. When maximum numbers are achieved it is possible that there may be small numbers north-west to Shropshire, but the woodlark has not been so far north for some fifty years, despite the fact that a marked maximum was reached in 1949–50. At the moment we seem to be emerging from a minimum number and the main areas of the woodlark are south Devon, south Somerset, the Brecklands, Suffolk and Norfolk. A modest number inhabit Hampshire, Surrey and Berkshire. The habitat favoured is well-treed open country, either where heathland borders more wooded land or where small, grazed fields have big hedges with many trees. Forest nurseries have sometimes been favourite places.

The CHAFFINCH is well known to have dialects which were important in the great days of caged wild song-birds. The London bird-catchers preferred Essex as a source of chaffinches because of the quality of their song. It is one of the songs known to be inherited rather than learned, and in a fairly sedentary species this state of affairs permits the emergence of regional fixed variation. The song of the chaffinch is a cheerful, rather brief burst of loud notes, almost a rattle, but just too musical to be so called, based on the call 'pink' or 'chink'. At the start it rapidly rises a little in pitch, but from there on, the dialects start. A good Essex bird then trills down the scale and ends with a clear flourish – 'chirrup-tu-weetchoo' whilst the poorest performers keep a 'chwinkchwinkchwink' on the same note and end in an indefinite 'chewee', more a fading away than a flourish. The average performer is somewhere in between; most dialect versions have a falling sequence but fewer have a good coda.

The chaffinch hit hard times in the south-east when seed-dressings of organic phosphates were widely used and by 1960 numbers were very low, especially in East Anglia. Since then there has been a recovery, slow in places but fair in others, and the bird is reasonably common in outer suburbs, towns and villages and on farmland and heath. The region which boosts the population to one of the largest of all the resident species is the birch-clad hillsides of vast areas of Scotland.

The notes of OWLS are imperfectly known. Their unique timbre is impossible to indicate in words and so are most of their utterances. Human vision is far more limited in even the brightest moonlight than is usually supposed. An owl calling in flight can sound, and may well be, close above the observer, but unless it should fly across the face of the moon it just will not be seen. At low levels of light at dusk and dawn the same is true, and even what we do see is seen in monochrome. Even the brightest moonlight does not allow us to see colours. Nearly as bad, and certainly completely unreliable, is the estimation of size and shape in half-light or less, and this is exacerbated by the sightings being almost invariably sudden, unexpected and partial. On one occasion two experienced observers walking back from watching by a marsh at dusk flushed a bird from the edge of a pond some fifteen yards away. One thought it probably a heron, the other was prepared to note it as a snipe.

Since the difficult owl-noises are those heard by night it is evident from the foregoing that resolving these is a considerable problem. Most owls do call by day or fly in daylight from time to time, but these occurrences are unhelpful. The tawny owl flies only when routed out of its roost by jays and a vociferous mob of tits, robins, blackbirds and dunnocks, but the owl remains silent. Tawny owls will hoot by day, quite frequently at around midday in deep, wooded, dark valleys, especially in Perthshire, but that hoot, in B-flat, is very well known already. Little owls give their 'kee-oo' call usually by day and often at intervals of a few minutes for hours, but are rarely or never seen making the variety of more interesting calls attributed to them. The barn owl floats about in daylight on summer or winter mornings and in summer evenings but is then quite silent. Similarly on a few chosen marshes, the isolated thorn-bush will in winter sometimes 'explode' with long-eared owls, but they are then silent. By night the barn and long-eared owls are credited with a wide variety of caterwauls and screechings, and written down it is difficult or impossible to differentiate among them.

The only ways to attribute purely nocturnal calls hitherto have been to await a lucky sighting, to keep one species in captivity and hope that it will use a range of notes, to listen within the vicinity of a known nest, and to listen for a long time in the hope that strange calls will be interspersed with known ones. One limitation to most of these methods (and it applies to taping calls too) is that it fails to distinguish between the sexes calling, and this is part of the problem. It is even thought that the female tawny owl may hoot and that the 'E-wick' call may be given at times by the male. Long series of taped calls would solve the problem of the inadequacy of written descriptions and, being repeatable, would allow some analysis of the calls and could make easier the hearing of known calls amongst the others.

The frequent occurrence of mimicry is mentioned in Chapter 2 and all sub-songs are worth recording, for they may well all contain some. The outpourings of the JAY are full of high-class mimicry, including animal noises, and seem little known. It must be rare for the chance of a recording to occur, for one very seldom hears it and then it is unexpected. Perhaps most likely in the breeding season, it has small carrying power and is done only when the bird is well inside thick cover. As soon as an approach is suspected the bird stops and may fly off.

The mimicry at the end of almost every song of the GOLDCREST is done so hurriedly that the unaided ear misses several components. Either the last phrase is over before it is identified or the more striking of two mimicries is recognized and the pleasure of recognition distracts the attention from the other, which is then missed. Taped songs can be repeated to overcome this second effect and slowed to overcome the first.

It would be fun to record all mimicking birds, to collect and list the repertoire of each species, and to find good performers to add new items to the lists. Little has been done to date on this, and pre-tape-recorder bird watchers were discouraged from reporting unexpected observations because of the impossibility of demonstrating them to unbelieving editors.

The above are but a few of the interesting possibilities open to the wildlife sound recordist.

10

Where and When to Record Mammals, Amphibians and Insects

MAMMALS

Mammal recordings are often difficult to obtain because it is not always possible to predict when they will vocalize. Many of them have a keen sense of smell which makes approach difficult and the majority are shy and retiring. Success is more certain to the recordist who makes a detailed study of his subject.

SQUIRRELS

Both the resident species, the red and the grey, can be very vocal but are more often seen than heard. The calls of the two species are very different.

Although the grey squirrel has been studied in some detail, very little has been written on the subject of vocalization and this is a good field for study. The author, along with many others, has spent hours trying to decipher the meaning of the calls without attaining very much success, although tape recordings have been made in every month of the year. From observation it has been found that the grey squirrel often calls while sitting on the bough of a tree, sometimes accompanied by vigorous tail jerking, and the calling will continue while it moves rapidly to a new position. The animal is quite at home in rural gardens and makes a very similar call after being chased by the household cat or dog. Whether the calls have any territorial significance is unknown but it is certain that vocalization is not confined to the breeding season.

The chatter comprises a number of short calls followed by longer, more drawn-out calls of approximately the same frequency. A study of the calls describes them as 'chucks' and 'squeals' and possibly the ratio of one to the other may have some significance. The ratio varies immensely and so does the speed of delivery. The drawn-out call (or the squeal) is sometimes preceded by a softer purring note thought to be caused by the teeth vibrating together. However, since the purr has been heard while the animal was holding a pine cone between the teeth, it could only be created by tongue and throat. There is also evidence of teeth chatter.

The grey squirrel makes various other sounds including short squeals when chasing each other, and if the drey can be located, usually a large untidy bundle of twigs high up in a tree, there is every chance at the right time of the year of obtaining family chatter. Once the grey squirrel has been heard calling it is possible that it will call continuously for ten minutes or even longer. During this time there is a good opportunity to make a reasonably close approach. Recordings from ten to twenty feet distance, using a reflector, produce the best results.

Since its introduction to this country the grey squirrel has increased rapidly and can now be found in nearly every English county. It is also spreading into Wales. So far, however, it does not seem to have reached the Lake District and parts of Norfolk. The habitat preferred is deciduous woodland but it is equally at home in pine forests.

The native red squirrel is still around in those areas of England where the grey has not yet arrived, although in some areas their ranges overlap. There are a number of red on Brownsea Island in Poole Harbour where they have escaped the disease now believed to be the major reason for their decline on the mainland. They can also be found in the northern areas of England, and the afforested areas of Scotland support a healthy population. Good red squirrel recordings are 'few and far between' and the call can only be described as plaintive squeals.

DEER

There are six species of deer living completely wild in the British Isles and all of them are good subjects for the recordist. It is interesting that in these days of ever increasing pressures on wildlife the deer population is increasing. Most of them are not truly native and like the grey squirrel have been purposely introduced for various reasons or are the result of escapes from deer parks.

Deer mainly vocalize during their period of rut. Red, fallow and roe are particularly noisy at this time. Good recordings can be made from a deer stalker's hide where the recordist must wait patiently.

The largest deer, the red, roam over Exmoor and the highlands of Scotland, and smaller numbers are present in the Lake District, the New Forest, the Midlands and in Kent, Sussex, Surrey and Norfolk. They are normally silent, but during the rut, which starts in October and continues for three or four weeks, the stag bellows or roars. The stag patrols his harem of hinds and roars defiance at any would-be interloper with whom he will fight with a mighty clashing of antlers. Occasionally the hind can be heard to emit a high-pitched whistle.

Witnessing these scenes in the wild requires a great deal of patience, and the animals require stalking which is a special skill. Fortunately there are many herds of red deer in deer parks such as Woburn and Lyme and there is no reason to believe that their behaviour is any different to those living completely wild. They are, however, a little easier to approach, which may be important if one is loaded with heavy equipment.

Fallow deer have now spread to nearly every English county and occur in smaller numbers in Scotland and Wales. Like the red, the bucks are very vocal during the rut which is usually a little later than the red deer rut. The buck produces a deep belching noise as he defends his harem, the does running around making a faint bleating sound. Again the clash of antlers as bucks spar with each other makes an interesting variation for the wildlife sound recordist. At the right time these scenes can be witnessed equally well in deer parks such as Petworth from which the local wild stock has been established from escapes.

Roe are very common over the whole of Scotland, English southern counties from Sussex to Dorset and in Norfolk. Smaller than the other two species mentioned, they are a great favourite with naturalists. The rut is towards the end of July but the buck is never particularly vocal, spending a great deal of time trotting behind his favourite doe. At this time the doe calls to attract the buck. Both sexes emit a characteristic warning bark, particularly if surprised by the observer before the animal has winded his approach.

The roe deer is much smaller than the red and fallow but has a vicious reputation. Deer when discovered usually retreat into hiding, but during the rut roebuck can suddenly turn and charge the observer.

The other three species, the sika, muntjac and Chinese water deer, are the result of more recent introductions and in consequence their numbers are small and extremely local. The sika is known in England and Scotland, a favourite place being parts of the New Forest. During October the sika's courting song, an almost blood-curdling scream, makes a thrilling subject for the recordist. The muntjac is well established in the Midlands and the recordist's interest is mainly in its alternative name, the barking deer. More local in the Midlands is the even smaller Chinese water deer.

F

RED FOX

The fox is a favourite subject and is common all over the British Isles. Vocalizations are many and varied and the best time for recording is during the fox rut from November to the end of January. The 'wow wow' call is usually attributed to the dog fox and the 'scream' to the vixen, although these calls are still the subject of investigation and may perhaps be made by either sex. The fox is nocturnal and this means that the best recording time is during the hours of darkness and often in the depths of winter! Fox recordings are often a matter of luck but it does help to know the habits of the fox population in your area. If the vixen's lair is found there is a possibility of recording cubs at play, but if disturbed the vixen will move the cubs. Probably the best technique is the reflector and at the lair an open microphone could be used.

BADGER

Badger watching is enjoyed by many naturalists and there is no reason why sound recording should not be attempted at the same time. Badgers are present in nearly every county of the British Isles and once an occupied set has been located the technique is to wait there at dusk, preferably downwind and in an elevated position. At dusk the observer will see the adults emerge although they may not remain long in the vicinity of the set. In April and May the young emerge for the first time and do not wander far away – this is the best time for recording at the set. It is then possible to obtain recordings of the parents and their young at play. At times the recordist may have to be satisfied with noises made by gathering bedding or be content to see the animals emerge noiselessly from their set and wander off in search of food. During the daytime a microphone lowered down the opening to an occupied set can produce a recording of snores from the occupants! Reflector or open microphone may be used.

OTHER MAMMALS

At the smaller end of the scale, shrews are extremely vocal, producing very high-pitched chattering that may well be inaudible to many ears. These sounds are difficult to record because of quick movement – sometimes the calls are too faint followed almost immediately by very loud calls.

Seals, otters, wild goats, wild ponies, weasels, stoats, etc. all present a further challenge to the wildlife sound recordist. Excursions can be planned in search of some of them, but recordings are often a matter of luck, being obtained accidentally whilst attempting to record other species. For example, whilst recording sea birds in Scotland or the Shetlands the whistling of otters or seals moaning is a thrilling possibility. On the other hand, a visit to the well-known breeding grounds of the grey seal on the Farne Islands should reward the recordist.

AMPHIBIANS

Vocal amphibians include the common frog and toad, the natterjack toad, the marsh frog and the edible frog. They all have their distinctive mating calls and it is interesting to collect them for comparison.

The common frog spawns quite early in the year from any time in February, again depending on the weather, and the would-be recordist must keep a good lookout if he is to succeed. The performance lasts only a day or two in a particular pond and may only be suitable for recording for a few hours. Common toads spawn a little later and the natterjack as late as May. The natterjack is not common but can be found in Lancashire and Surrey – it is protected by law and it is illegal to pick one up. The natterjack toad and the marsh frog are easy to record as their calls are loud, but the common frog and common toad (particularly the toad) call relatively softly and it is usually difficult to obtain a satisfactory signal.

INSECTS

Collecting the sounds of grasshoppers and crickets may not be everyone's idea of pleasure, but they present a real challenge to the recordist. They all produce quite distinctive sounds, many of them stridulating at such a high frequency that the sounds may not be audible to human ears. The best time for such an expedition is in August or September, and as bird song at that time is almost non-existent, the recordist can at least be content in knowing that he is not missing any great opportunities in that direction. Identifying the species presents some problems and many prefer to capture a specimen before they can be sure. Capturing the insects may well be the only way to secure satisfactory recordings as they can then be placed in a heated container and recorded in the relative peace and quiet of the home. The insects need a temperature of 65–70°F to start stridulating. Overheating will harm them and they should, of course, be returned to the place where they were captured as soon as possible.

Further reading

BURROWS, R., *Wild Fox*, David and Charles, 1968.

Forestry Commission, *Badgers in Woodlands*, Leaflet No. 34, HMSO.

Forestry Commission, *The Fallow Deer*, Leaflet No. 5, HMSO.

Forestry Commission, *The Roe Deer*, Leaflet No. 45, HMSO.

NEAL, E., *The Badger*, New Naturalist Series, Collins, 1969.

PRIOR, R., *Living with Deer*, Survival Books, André Deutsch, 1965.

RAGGE, D. R., *Grasshoppers, Crickets and Cockroaches of the British Isles*, Wayside and Woodland Series, Warne, 1965.

SHORTEN, M., *Squirrels*, New Naturalist Series, Collins, 1954.

SMITH, M., *The British Amphibians and Reptiles*, New Naturalist Series, Collins, 1969.

VAN DEN BRINK, F. H., *A Field Guide to the Mammals of Britain and Europe*, Collins, 1967.

The Studio

Work in the studio begins before a recording expedition and ends with the preparation of copies for any particular purpose.

PREPARATION FOR FIELDWORK

The equipment must be checked at home to make sure that it is in full working order. Microphone leads, which can be troublesome, must be inspected to make sure that all connections are in perfect condition. A spare set of leads should also be included to cover unforeseen accidents.

Batteries are an important item. If rechargeable cells are used, make sure they are fully charged before leaving. If, however, there is any doubt about a mains supply being available while you are away it is better not to take rechargeable cells as it is harmful to leave them for any length of time in a discharged condition.

Replacement cells should be checked before being put into the recorder because even new cells are not always perfect. They may have been in stock for some time before they were purchased. New cells should have an open circuit voltage of about 1.65 volts and should be capable of delivering well over one amp when short-circuited. A short-circuit test may seem rather drastic and, of course, should only be maintained long enough to show that the discharge will exceed one amp.

An adequate supply of recording tape must not be over-looked because suitable tape on the right size of spool could be unobtainable in the area of operation and could be un-economic. Tape is generally cheaper on 180 mm spools, and although some portables will take this size of spool, most portables are only suitable for spools up to 130 mm diameter. For field use it therefore pays the majority of recordists to purchase tape on 180 mm spools and rewind on to smaller spools. The surplus 180 mm spools can be used for storing finished recordings. When tape has been respooled it will be found an added advantage to leave a leader on one end only so that a used spool can be instantly recognized and the disaster of recording over material you wish to save can be avoided. In bad light a red leader can often be confused with tape and therefore should be avoided. White or yellow leaders show more clearly in these conditions.

Tape that has been used before should have all traces of previous recordings removed. The cleaning of tapes can be done on the recorder but a bulk eraser is more efficient and much faster. Recording over previous recordings can lead to confusion on playback when snatches of old record-ings appear in the gaps between new ones. It is also much easier to recognize the end of a new recording when a trial playback is made in the field.

EDITING

All recordings should be edited as soon as possible after returning home. It is irritating to listen to wildlife sounds accompanied by a commentary from the recordist to the effect that 'there's a good bit coming'. Only the good recordings should be retained and the remainder bulk-erased.

In the spring when field activity is usually at its peak

there is often insufficient time to edit all tapes from one excursion before the next one takes place. Inevitably, there is a build-up of tapes awaiting editing, but it is unwise to leave all tapes to be edited for the winter months as the task may well have become formidable. It is also obvious that such a procedure would involve the use of a much greater amount of tape to cover a season's activities than is necessary.

There are two basic methods of editing, the first being to use an exclusive copying process sometimes referred to as panel editing, and the second (more commonly used) being to cut and splice the original.

Some recordists use the copying method only as it has the merit of retaining the original recording in an untouched state. As only extracts of a maximum duration of two to three minutes (often much shorter) are required, direct copying can produce an infinite number of different copies. However, retaining all original recordings can present problems of expense and storage.

The copying method obviously requires the use of two recorders, or at least one recorder and a playback deck. The field recorder could be used as the playback deck but the copying machine must have interjection facilities if the method is used exclusively. The method is simple enough if the piece to be copied does not contain any extraneous noise and is therefore a straightforward copying process.

The material to be copied is placed on one recorder or the playback deck and the recording is played until the beginning and end of the part to be copied are located. Notes are made of the machine's counter at these positions and the tape is rewound to the beginning. The second machine is then loaded with new tape and appropriate transfer connections are made. Select this machine to the record mode and play the extract again, adjusting the gain control by referring to the VU meter. A note is then made of the maximum gain setting thus obtained which is then returned to zero and the original tape is again rewound to the beginning. The playback machine is now started followed by the copying machine as soon after as possible and the gain control smoothly rotated to the setting previously noted. This will produce a nice fade-in to the copy and should last not more than a second, or else the listener will become impatient. About two seconds from the end of the selected piece the gain control is smoothly rotated to zero and the machines are stopped. The copy can then be checked to make sure it has not been over-modulated, and finally leaders may be added.

If the piece to be copied contains some extraneous noise which has to be eliminated during the copying, the process becomes more complicated. The first requirement already referred to is that the copying machine must have inter-jection facilities. That is to say, it can be switched from playback to record without having to stop the tape trans-port during the process.

Let us suppose that between two bursts of song there is a nearby gun shot and it is wished to remove this during the copying process. As soon as the sound is heard on the loudspeaker both machines are stopped as soon as possible. A note is made of the position indicator of the copying machine and the tape is rewound a few feet. Both machines are now set in motion but this time the copying machine is started in the playback mode. Just before the indicator of the copying machine reaches the previously noted reading of the position indicator it is switched into the record mode and the machine continues to copy the original after the gunshot sound has passed. It may all sound very simple, but timing is most important to make sure that the copying machine is not dropped into the record mode in the middle of a burst of song from the original.

The more popular method of editing is to actually cut the tape. A portable machine may be used but the duty is very severe involving a great deal of stopping, starting and winding in both directions. A mains machine is more robust and its winding is generally much faster.

The first step in editing in this manner is to listen carefully to the tape, noting the rough positions of those parts you wish to keep. Then rewind the tape and mark the commencement of the first section with a chinagraph pencil. If possible this is done by marking the tape as it lies on the playback head, but it may be necessary to pull back a pressure pad or mu-metal screen to obtain access. The mark should be made on line with the gap in the head. On some machines access to the heads is impossible without completely dismantling the machine, and in these cases the tape must be marked as it passes over some nearby tape guide. If the tape is marked against the playback head it can be pressed into the splicing block with the mark lined up exactly with the cutting slot in the block. If it is necessary to mark the tape elsewhere, it is a good idea to mount the splicing block permanently on the deck and make a mark on the deck exactly the same distance from the cutting slot as the tape head gap is from the guide used for marking the tape.

Whichever method of marking is used, the tape can be cut precisely. The right-hand spool can now be removed from the machine and the tape to the right-hand side of the cut removed from the splicing block at the same time. Take about 300 mm of leader tape and lay one end just over the slot of the splicing block to replace the tape just removed. Draw the razor blade across the slot again thus trimming the leader and leaving the tape and leader accurately butting up to each other. Join them by using about 25 mm of splicing tape and remove from the block. Then dust with french chalk. Put a spare empty reel on the right-hand hub and rethread the tape.

Now continue to play the recording until the end of the extract is reached. For the present ignore any extraneous noises. At the end of the extract stop the machine, mark the tape, cut it and add a length of leader in a similar manner to that described for the beginning. Remove the right-hand spool and identify it, using a self-adhesive label. Replace the original right-hand spool and, using the splicing block, join up the two ends of the tape. Then, assuming there are no more extracts to be taken from this spool, rewind it to the left-hand spool which can then be bulk-erased and returned to stock.

The process of splicing takes less time than its description, but is the whole basis of this form of editing.

Before copies can be made for any given purpose it is necessary to remove those little irritating plops caused by handling and any other unnatural sounds, and the extracts must now be fine-edited. If the extract contains many imperfections, fine editing can be very time-consuming and it may be preferable to file the extract untouched and hope for another opportunity to record the same subject. It is, however, a useful exercise to edit a poor recording of a common species so that when it becomes necessary to edit a recording of a rare species, the recording of which cannot be so easily repeated, the work can be tackled with confidence.

To fine-edit play the tape in the normal way until the start of the first blemish is heard and then stop the machine instantly. With the machine still in the playback mode, rotate the spools by hand in a clockwise direction. The unwanted noise is then heard backwards and at a reduced frequency, but if the spools are handled skilfully, rocking back and forth, it will be found that the start can be located to within a fraction of an inch. Mark the tape just before the noise commences. If the noise stops within 50 to 150 mm, find the exact end and again mark the tape. The remainder of the exercise consists of removing the short length of tape between the two marks, using the splicing block, and joining up the two lengths of tape.

A quick check on the result should reveal that the blemish has disappeared without trace. If a somewhat longer length of tape has to be removed, it is better to cut the tape after making the first mark, so that the mark will not be lost. Continue to play the tape, allowing the unwanted portion to spool up on a spare spool or simply to shoot out on to the floor. When the noise ends, stop the machine immediately and again locate the exact end by manual manipulation of the spools. Mark, cut and splice up to the original tape as before, and with a bit of luck all the noise will have disappeared. This time the splice may be noticeable, owing to the fact that with the lapsed time the ambience may have changed. In this case there is no option but to try discarding a little more tape in the hope that the ambience will match. A sudden change in ambience can often be less noticeable if the two ambiences are separated by a song phrase.

All the foregoing must, of course, be related to the actual subject of the recording. For example, the repertoire of a wren is fairly short but to a specific pattern. If some handling noise occurs during one phrase the complete phrase must be cut out or the edit will be noticeable.

Editing is an art and practice leads to perfection. Each cut and its probable effect must be considered before starting to edit. Of course, the better the field work the less editing is required.

After fine-editing we should have an apparently continuous flawless recording lasting perhaps five to ten minutes.

Cassette recordings present a special problem. The direct copying technique is probably the best method as the actual cutting and splicing of a cassette tape with accuracy is virtually impossible. If the copying machine does not possess interjection facilities, the only solution is to copy the whole of the cassette, or at least selected parts, and then fine-edit the copy by cutting. Final copies made for presentation will, therefore, be one more generation removed from the original.

During editing by the copying process or in preparing copies from a cut-edited original, the signal may be further processed by filtering or by other means, and the dubbing amplifier shown in Figs 16(a) and 16(b) is a useful accessory for this purpose. For simplicity the circuit is shown in mono form, but it can be produced in stereo form if required with controls for both channels being ganged for convenience of operation.

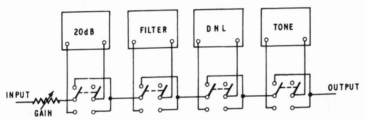

Fig. 16(a) Line diagram of dubbing amplifier

The amplifier consists of four sections which by virtue of the switches can be used individually or in any combination, but if more than one section is in use the signal is routed through them in a prescribed order. If desired, the sections can be built as separate modules so that they may be added at different times as the need arises. The first section consists of a high-quality 20 dB amplifier recommended by Mullard. This is useful for boosting weak signals. The main gain control allows slightly stronger signals to be reduced so that the amplifier is not overloaded. If the signal is even stronger, the stage can be bypassed.

The second section comprises a two-stage active bass cut filter specially developed by John Kirby for processing wildlife sound recordings. The use of such a filter was briefly referred to in Chapter 3. This filter incorporates a nine-position switch, eight of which give a 10 dB per

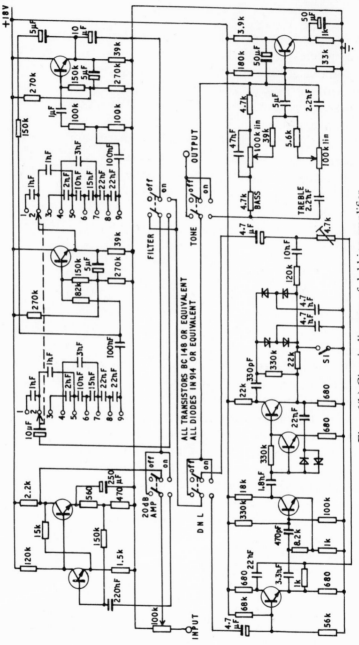

Fig. 16(b) Circuit diagram of dubbing amplifier

octave bass cut, each one starting at progressively higher frequencies. The first position is substantially flat, and theoretically the switch can be left in this position when filtering is not required, but under these conditions it is better to use the main switch so that the section is completely bypassed.

The filter is particularly useful in reducing noise emanating from aircraft and motor vehicles, but even these sources contain frequencies overlapping those of many wildlife species, so care must be taken to select a switch position that does not affect the wanted signal. Thus the filter is not a miraculous cure for noise and although it can bring about a very acceptable improvement, it cannot substitute for a recording made under more ideal conditions.

The third section consists of a Dynamic Noise Limiter (DNL) as developed by Philips. The theory of operation was given briefly in Chapter 4 from which it will be appreciated that true signals of similar frequency to those caused by tape hiss must be of much greater magnitude if they are not to be eliminated as well. The circuit is, therefore, somewhat critical and for best results requires careful regulation of signal strength. Perhaps its best application is for use in dubbing from cassette to standard tape when the hiss for which cassette machines are more renowned can be reduced considerably. To check the correct functioning of the DNL, advance the main gain control as far as possible without the onset of audible distortion and compare the sound with S1 open and closed. When S1 is closed the DNL feature is temporarily removed and the improvement should be apparent. Preset 4K7 is set to produce minimum hiss conditions and requires no further adjustment after initial setting up.

Last but not least, the fourth section adds bass and treble controls to a circuit recommended by Mullard. These controls can be used for a number of applications.

If the filter section is in use at the same time, the bass frequencies will already have been progressively reduced. In consequence the bass tone control is largely ineffective, but under these circumstances the treble control will be found useful to restore the overall frequency balance. If the filter section is not in use, the controls can be used to create a more pleasant sound, although theoretically the section should be bypassed. One further application is to compensate for different recording characteristics. As explained in Chapter 4, if the time constants of the machine used to make the original recording are different from those of the machine on which the recording is replayed, the sound will be over-brilliant, or dull, depending on whether the playback time constant is lower or higher than on the record machine. For all practical purposes the tone controls, particularly the treble control, can compensate for this difference.

With the foregoing notes the use of the amplifier should be apparent. The recording to be copied should be replayed a number of times using the copying recorder as an amplifier and the effect of the dubbing amplifier should be studied. During this process the tone controls on the copying recorder must be set level because they will also affect the quality of the reproduced sound when used as a straight-through amplifier although they are ineffective during recording. When the operator is satisfied that the dubbing amplifier is correctly adjusted, the copy may proceed as already described.

Finally, at the same time as making the copy, a spoken commentary can be mixed in with the signal. Opinions vary considerably, some feeling that if a commentary is required the spoken words should finish before the wildlife sound commences.

COPYING TROUBLES

Making a good copy of a natural history recording is not always an easy task, although with the right technique and equipment a copy can always be made which the ear can scarcely distinguish from the original.

A copy must inevitably have a worse signal-to-noise ratio than the original but this deterioration can be kept to the minimum by using the fastest speed on the copying deck that is available.

Over-modulation distortion can occur in exactly the same way as it does when using the field recorder and microphone. As usual, the reason is that the response time of the VU meter is much longer than the signal duration with the result that the true signal strength is never seen. The only advantage when making a copy is that the process can be repeated until exactly the right gain setting is found.

There is another form of distortion which produces an audible effect similar to over-modulation and is thought to be caused by an elastic stretching of the tape between the pay-off and take-up spools. On a portable the free length of tape is usually quite short compared with mains machines and this probably explains why a portable will often make a better copy than a mains machine. The effect can be practically eliminated by fitting extra idler pulleys known as scrape rollers as close to the head block assembly as possible. Even one roller can have a marked effect. The rollers must be free to turn as the tape passes over them and yet stiff enough to introduce some drag. Many manufacturers are now incorporating rollers on their standard products.

STORING AND INDEXING RECORDINGS

A growing collection of recordings presents storing and indexing problems. It is hardly necessary to point out that precious recordings should not be left around indefinitely to collect dust, become lost or suffer damage. Recordings should be returned to their boxes and kept in a warm dry room and obviously well away from stray magnetic fields such as loudspeakers and microphones etc.

As each spool of tape is edited some means must be found whereby the cuts to be saved can be stored and found easily when required. Many beginners file all their recordings in chronological order, which makes it difficult to find particular recordings for comparison. If expense and space are no object, however, a separate spool could be allocated to every species.

There are innumerable ways of filing recordings and the author commends his own method as one that is not expensive to implement and yet can be expanded indefinitely as the collection grows, with the minimum amount of reorganization.

Recordings of birds are the most numerous and it was decided to file these recordings in the accepted family order familiar to ornithologists. A comprehensive listing of European species is given in F. H. Van Der Brink's *A Field Guide to the Birds of Britain and Europe* published by Collins. The guide gives a list of families commencing with divers and ending with crows, making a total of sixty families. Recordings of some species within these families, such as pelicans and orioles, are likely to be uncommon and therefore, initially, it is not even necessary to devote a separate spool to each family. Accordingly it was decided to group several families together to form one category, reducing the sixty families into twenty-five categories. A separate spool was then devoted to each category. As the collection expands, the number of reels devoted to each category will increase and each can be reorganized without affecting adjoining categories.

For example, if Category 23 were chosen to cover two families, say finches and buntings, initially recordings of any species within these families would be filed on the same spool. When the spool is full it would be a convenient time to break it down into separate families so that the first spool labelled C23–1 would hold finch recordings and C23–2 would hold bunting recordings. As reel C23–1 is filled it is time to further break it down into species so that C23–1–A covers greenfinches, C23–1–B covers goldfinches, etc. At a later date, if a single species expands on to two spools these would become C23–1–A–1 and C23–1–A–2.

In parallel with filing the recordings a reliable method of keeping records is required. A loose-leaf file is the answer to this problem. The first page will form an index and thereafter a separate sheet is required for each spool, carrying the same number as the spool. The various cuts are then listed in playing sequence giving details of species, duration of recording, place and date of recording, and equipment used. Additional columns can be included for other information such as the time of the recording and the weather conditions if the recordist feels these are significant. Each time a category is reorganized it means rewriting the sheets and destroying the old ones. It is therefore better to leave any reorganization to winter months and to place the current season's recordings on holding spools.

Appendix 1 – Protected Birds

PROTECTION OF BIRDS ACTS 1954–1967 (ENGLAND, SCOTLAND AND WALES), SCHEDULE 1 (BIRDS)

It is an offence to wilfully disturb any wild bird on the Schedule 1 list whilst it is on or near its nest.

PART I (PROTECTED AT ALL TIMES)

Avocet
Bee-eater, all species
Bittern, all species
Bluethroat
Brambling
Bunting, snow
Buzzard, honey
Chough
Corncrake
Crake, spotted
Crossbill
Diver, all species
Dotterel
Eagle, all species
Fieldfare
Firecrest
Godwit, blacktailed
Goshawk
Grebe, black-necked
Grebe, Slavonian
Greenshank
Harrier, all species
Hobby
Hoopoe
Kingfisher
Kite
Merlin
Oriole, golden
Osprey
Owl, barn
Owl, snowy
Peregrine
Phalarope, red-necked
Plover, Kentish
Plover, little ringed
Quail, European

Redstart, black
Redwing
Ruff and reeve
Sandpiper, wood
Serin
Shrike, red-backed
Sparrowhawk
Spoonbill
Stilt, black-winged
Stint, Temminck's
Stone curlew

Swan, whooper
Tern, black
Tern, little
Tern, roseate
Tit, bearded
Tit, crested
Warbler, Dartford
Warbler, Marsh
Warbler, Savi's
Woodlark
Wryneck

PART II (PROTECTED DURING THE CLOSE-SEASON)

Whimbrel
Wild duck of the following species:
    Common scoter
    Garganey teal
    Goldeneye
    Long-tailed duck
    Scaup-duck
    Velvet Scoter

Appendix 2 – Technical Terms

In writing this book it has been assumed that the reader has a fundamental knowledge of electrical terms and other reference works may be consulted for a detailed explanation. The following summary may, however, be of some assistance.

Direct current (*DC*) such as provided by the batteries of a tape recorder flows continuously in one direction. The current (*I*) is measured in amperes usually abbreviated to amps. In tape recorders the currents are often relatively small and the terms milliamp (mA) and microamp (μA) being a thousandth and a millionth of an amp are frequently used.

Alternating current (*AC*) flows in alternate directions, changing direction in accordance with its stated frequency (*f*). Electricity in our homes changes direction fifty times a second but the AC current generated in a microphone changes direction as often as the alternating sound pressures acting on its diaphragm. Therefore, in audio work we meet alternating currents of the same frequency as all those in the normal sound spectrum.

An *electrical circuit* comprises one or more components through which the current flows. The size of the current depends on the ability of the circuit to impede its flow and on the amount of pressure applied to force the current through.

The *electrical pressure* (*E*) is measured in volts (*V*) and smaller units such as the millivolt (mV) and microvolt

(μV) are commonly used. The impedance of the circuit
(Z) is measured in ohms and according to Ohm's Law
$$I = \frac{E}{Z}.$$

There are basically three types of *components* used in
an electrical circuit, namely *resistors*, *capacitors* and *inductors* (often taking the form of coils such as oscillator or
head coils).

The size of a *resistor* (R) is measured in ohms and can
be regarded as constant whether the current is DC or AC.

The size of a *capacitor* (C) is measured in farads (F),
microfarads (μF), nano-farads (nF) or pico-farads (pF).

Basically, a capacitor comprises two metal plates insulated from each other and, therefore, cannot pass a DC
current. However, an AC current effectively flows through
a capacitor and its ability to restrict the flow is termed
capacitive reactance (X_C) and is measured in ohms. The
capacitive reactance depends not only on the capacitor size
but also on the frequency. Thus $X_C = \frac{1}{Cf}$.

The size of an inductor (L) is measured in henries (H)
and to an AC current it presents an *inductive reactance*
(X_L) measured in ohms and again dependent on the frequency. Thus $X_L = Lf$.

The *impedance* (Z) of a circuit is, therefore, an arithmetical computation of all the resistances (R), capacitive
reactances (X_C) and inductive reactances (X_L). It will be
noted that the impedance will vary with frequency and,
therefore, an AC current can vary in magnitude even with
the same set of components.

Power is measured in watts (W) and again the smaller
unit milliwatt (mW) is frequently used. It is derived from
the product of the square of the current (I) and the
resistance (R) of the load.

A *diode* is a solid-state device which will pass current
in one direction only. Thus if an AC pressure is applied,

when the pressure reverses no current will flow. Under these circumstances it is often termed a rectifier and is purposely used to convert an AC signal into a DC signal of corresponding value.

A *transistor* is a current amplifying static device, many different types being available, some being low power/high power gain with very low noise, such as used in microphone and head preamplifiers, others being designed to deliver power sufficient to drive large loudspeakers.

Index

Ambience, 156
Ambisonic, 133, 134
Amphibians, 147
Automatic gain control, 78
Automatic noise reduction system
   (ANRS), 80

Badger, 146
Balanced lines, 58
Bar, 46
Bass cut filter, 44, 157
Bass roll-off, 44
Batteries, 64, 83, 84, 150
Bell, Alexander Graham, 43
Bias, 75, 76
Binoculars, 108
Bird families, 162
Bird song, developed, 31
   highly developed, 33
   mechanical, 36
   mimicry, 36, 140
   partially developed, 29
   primitive, 27
Bittern, 28
Blackbird, 16, 33, 123
Blackcap, 33, 37
Blue tit, 37
Boosting weak signals, 157
BSI standards, 73
Bulk eraser, 151
Bullfinch, 31
Bunting, cirl, 28
   corn, 28
   reed, 28, 33

Call down, 119
Capstan, 62, 63
Cartridge, 60
Cassette, machines, 82, 83
   recording, 82
   system, 59
Cassettes, pre-recorded, 15, 59
CCIR standards, 73
Chaffinch, 29, 37, 138
Chiffchaff, 25, 27
Chinagraph pencil, 154
Clothing, 109
Coal tit, 37
Collins, 162
Competitions, 17, 18
Corncrake, 38
Crickets, 148
Crossbill, 30
Cuckoo, 27

Dawn chorus, 15
Dan Gibson, 98
Decibel, 43
Deer, 144, 145
Dialect, 8, 16, 17, 136
DIN standards, 73
Dipper, 31, 38
Divided reflector, 130
Dolby, 78, 79, 80
Drop out, 69
Dubbing amplifier, 157
Dunnock, 32, 38
Dynamic noise limiter (DNL), 80,
   159

Dyne, 46

Ear, 44
Earpiece, 107
EBU, 18
Editing, 69, 151–6
Editing deck, 85
EMI L4, 83
Erase head, 64, 65, 76
Equalization, 73
Eye, 21

Farnell Tandberg, 13
Ferrograph, 86
Field effect transistor, 49
Field techniques, 111
Fieldwork, 150
Filtering, 121, 157, 159, 160
Flutter, 60, 61, 63
Flutter echo, 128
Fox, 146
French chalk, 154
Frensham Great Pond, 34
Frequency response, 42, 45, 47, 65, 66
Frog, 147
Full track recording, 66

Gain control, 72
Goat, 147
Goldcrest, 27, 29, 140
Goldfinch, 30, 34, 38
Grampian, 97, 98
Grasshoppers, 148
Great tit, 16, 37
Greenfinch, 28, 30, 33
Grundig, 83

Half-track recording, 66
Hawfinch, 29
Headgap, 65, 66, 154
Headlift preamplifier, 76
Headphones, 101, 107
Hearing, 23, 24
Hides, 118
Housemartin, 32, 33

Hum, 57

Indexing recordings, 161
Insects, 104, 148

Jay, 37, 38
JVC, 83

Kingfisher, 30
Kirby, John, 157
Koch, Ludwig, 59

Lapwing, 27
Limiters, 81
Linnet, 32, 33, 34
Little grebe, 27
Loudspeaker, 60

3M Co., 13
Mains recorder, 64, 85, 116, 117
Mammals, 142
Marsh tit, 26, 37
Meadow pipit, 26, 30
Microphone, balance, 129
    bass response, 53
    capacitor, 39, 40, 41, 42, 45, 48, 49, 50, 52, 53
    cardioid, 51, 52, 96, 115
    choice, 115, 116
    directional characteristic, 51
    dynamic, 39, 40, 45, 47, 49, 50, 52, 53
    electret, 41
    electrostatic, 39
    gun, 51, 52, 55, 113, 130
    impedance matching, 56
    leads, 53, 55, 56, 57, 58, 117, 150
    matching transformer, 56, 58
    moving coil, 41, 42
    noise, 45, 48, 49
    omni, 51, 52, 92, 97, 115
    open, 114, 115
    preamplifier, 58, 72, 104–7
    resilient mounts, 55, 54
    response curves, 53
    sensitivity, 45, 48

Microphone—*cont.*
  shape, 52
  signal-to-noise, 49
  specification, 41
  stethoscope, 133
  technique, 111
  weight, 52
  wind shields, 52, 53, 54, 55
Mimicry, 34, 36, 37, 38, 140
Modulation, 124
Monitoring, 117, 118
Monopod, 112, 113
Mullard, 157, 159
Multitrack recorder, 131
Multitrack recording, 132

Nagra, 82, 83
Nakamichi, 83
NARTB (NAB) standards, 73, 74
Newton, 46
Nightingale, 35
Nightjar, 28
Noise, aircraft, 159
  background, 121
  handling, 99, 100, 112, 121
  mechanical, 112
  motor-vehicle, 159
Noise reduction systems, 59, 69,
    77
Nuthatch, 29, 37

Oscillator, 65, 75, 76
Otter, 147
Overmodulation, 124, 161
Owl, 34, 139, 140
Oystercatcher, 27

Pascal, 46
Patchett, Prof. G. N., 92–8
Peak programme meter (PPM),
    74, 75
Permanent magnet, 65
Pheasant, 28
Philips, 59, 159
Pigeon, 28
Pinch roller, 62, 63

Playback, head, 55, 66, 154
  howl, 122
  preamplifier, 86
Pony, 147
Portable, cassette recorder, 59
  reel-to-reel recorder, 59
Pressure pads, 63, 154

Quadrophony, 133, 134
Quail, 27
Quarter-track recording, 67, 68

Radio interference, 57
Record head, 65, 66
Recorder, balanced input, 58
  basic components, 60
  belt-drive, 62
  brakes, 62
  carrying case, 84
  controls, 62, 84
  field, 81
  flywheel, 63
  gain control, 72, 124
  monitoring facilities, 85
  motors, 62, 63, 64
  playing speed, 60, 61, 64
  preamplifier, 60, 65, 70, 71, 72,
    107
  selection, 81
  servo, 64
  solenoid, 62
  speed control, 64
  tacho-generator, 64
  take-up spool, 63
  tape transport, 60, 61
  tracks, 66, 67, 68, 69
  weight, 84
Recording, amphibians, 116
  evaluation, 123, 124
  insects, 104, 116, 148
  systems, 69
Red-backed shrike, 32
Redpoll, 30
Redshank, 25
Redstart, 31, 38
Reel-to-reel recording, 82

Reflector, focal length, 95, 97
  graphics, 91
  handle, 99, 100
  microphone mount, 99, 100
  peephole, 101
  sights, 102
  technique, 111
  weight, 99
  windshield, 102, 103
Reslo Sound, 98
Revox, 86
Ringed plover, 30
Robin, 35, 37, 74, 124

Sandpiper, 28
Sandwich tern, 16
Scrape rollers, 161
Seal, 147
Shrew, 147
Signal-to-noise, 66, 71, 107, 161
Siskin, 30
Skeel, Jack, 13
Skylark, 27, 37, 112
Snipe, 29, 36
Sonic Instruments, 98
Sony, 83
Sound spectrogram, 17
Sparrow, 29
Splicing, 155
Splicing block, 154, 155
Squirrel, 142, 143
Starling, 34, 36, 135, 136, 137
Stereo, field checks, 131
  microphone technique, 128,
    129, 130
  recording, 55, 67, 126, 127
  recordings, 131
Stockdove, 27
Stone curlew, 22
Stonechat, 32, 38
Storing recordings, 162
Swallow, 32, 34, 38
Swift, 27

Tandberg, 82, 83
Tape, cassette, 87

chromium dioxide, 85, 87
  compensation, 72
  copying, 152, 156, 157, 161
  equalizing, 73
  guide, 63, 154
  leaders, 151
  long play, 87
  low noise, 69
  non-ferric oxide, 59
  sandwich, 85
  storage, 162, 163
Tape deck, 60
Thermionic valve, 59
Thrush, 31, 37
Time constants, 73
Toad, 147
Tombs, David J., 129
Tone controls, 160
Transistor, 59
Tree pipit, 26, 30
Tree sparrow, 33
Treecreeper, 27, 30

Uher, 82, 83, 84

Van Der Brink, F. H., 162
VU meter, 74, 75, 100, 101, 124,
    152, 161

Wagtail, 22, 30, 38
Wahlstrom, Sten, 130
Warbler, Dartford, 32
  garden, 33, 37, 38
  grasshopper, 28
  great reed, 33
  marsh, 34, 37
  reed, 33, 37
  Savi's, 29
  sedge, 37
  willow, 25, 29
  wood, 25, 29
Water rail, 28
Wax cylinder, 59
Wax disc, 59
Weasel, 147
Wheatear, 32, 38

Whimbrel, 28

Whinchat, 32, 38

White, Gilbert, 25

Whitethroat, 31, 33, 37

Wildlife Sound Recording Society, 11, 18

Willow tit, 26

Wind, 122

Windshield, 52, 54, 103, 122

Wire recorder, 59

Woodcock, 28

Woodpecker, 26, 27, 29, 36

Wow, 60, 61, 63

Wren, 17, 31, 74, 156

Yellowhammer, 28